Botanic Gems
Indiana Public Gardens

INCLUDING
GREATER CHICAGO, DAYTON, CINCINNATI & LOUISVILLE

ALAN McPHERSON

AuthorHouse™
1663 Liberty Drive
Bloomington, IN 47403
www.authorhouse.com
Phone: 1-800-839-8640

As a legal disclaimer, the author is not held responsible for accidents that may incur en route to or at a garden site mentioned herein. The reader must accept full responsibility for any accident or injury that may incur while using this guide.

First published by AuthorHouse 7/22/2009

ISBN: 978-1-4343-7772-2 (sc)

Printed in the United States of America
Bloomington, Indiana

This book is printed on acid-free paper.

Front Cover: White River Gardens, Indianapolis
Back Cover, L-R: Floral Clock, Lakeside Park, Fort Wayne
              Potawatomi Park Conservatories, South Bend
              T.C. Steele Gardens, Belmont
Title Page: Sunken Gardens, Lakeside Park, Fort Wayne

authorHOUSE®

PREFACE

"The more beautiful a garden can be made, the greater the testimonial to the kind and quality of heart...."
Gene Stratton-Porter

"The [garden] work entailed was hard, but if the heart is in it, the air is full of song."
Selma Steele

Indiana is a garden, a state where horticultural pursuits are richly rewarded. Botanic knowledge, hard work and the right combination of natural "ingredients" such as ample moisture, a long, frost-free growing season, and fertile soil adds up to creating beautiful gardens. The love of gardening is widely reflected in our numerous private and public gardens. Personal and public involvement in gardening has been steadily increasing.

In my travels across Indiana and neighboring metropolitans such as Greater Chicago, Dayton, Cincinnati and Louisville, I have visited numerous public gardens that are described and illustrated in the following pages. The project involved a considerable amount of research, travel, photography, checking information, consultation and correspondence. To my knowledge, no other guidebook of Indiana's public gardens has been published. This compilation of public gardens is one way of thanking those responsible for these "botanic gems" and informing the public where they may be found and enjoyed.

For those interested in the public gardens of our region they will find this resource offers substantial information. The main section features forty-two botanic sites that are arranged geographically. An alphabetical listing of other significant Hoosier public gardens follows the main text. A third section is devoted to the first class public gardens of Indiana's neighboring metropolitans such as Greater Chicago, Dayton, Cincinnati and Louisville, all within a day's drive. I have attempted via words and photographs to retain the spirit of beauty and love of nature each garden imparts. The accompanying highway maps guide you there.

The author would like to thank the numerous individuals and institutions that have contributed their energy to this compendium. It would be a challenging task to name all those to whom gratitude is due. Especial thanks to my supporting family and personal friend, Renate, who often accompanied me on many garden sojourns. A deep debt of gratitude goes to graphic designers, Matthew Wilson, who spent many hours designing the maps and Robert DeGroff, who designed the manuscript into book form.

For those interested in where the most outstanding botanical garden gems in Hoosierdom are located, you are holding the answer in your hands. Take this guidebook, friends, and go!

CONTENTS

Sunken Garden, West Baden Springs

WELCOME

"Indiana.........is a garden
Where the seeds of peace have grown,
Where each tree, and vine, and flower
Have a beauty.....all its own."

Arthur Franklin Mapes

You may inquire of any visitor to a public garden why they seek out such places and their most common response is beauty and the uplifting joy and delight that flowers and plants impart. As the modern world becomes more complex and further removed from nature, the simple pleasure of enjoying lush green places becomes increasingly necessary. Seeking God in nature fulfills a deep spiritual desire for an Eden-like earthly paradise.

Now more than ever, an increasing number of people are visiting public gardens and creating their own personal gardens. Today, Indiana residents and visitors are fortunate in having a growing number of public accessible botanic sites to explore and enjoy. This informative guide book has located the best public gardens, including arboretums and conservatories, to visit in Indiana and neighboring cities of Chicago, Dayton, Cincinnati, and Louisville.

The public gardens herein were selected for their beauty, design, botanic collections, historic significance, mission, unique elements, educational commitment, availability and permanence. The botanic sites are arranged in a geographical sequence, from north to south in the state of Indiana. The top forty-plus public gardens feature a color photo(s), brief text profile, and maps. Late April through October is considered the ideal time of year for garden visitation; however, the winter season has its moments of beauty and interest.

Each featured public garden has its unique landscaping style. The garden designs of England, France, Italy and Japan as well as American Colonial and Prairie styles have greatly influenced the designs of Hoosier public gardens.

History and purpose has also played a major role in garden layout. There are estate gardens (Oakhurst, Oldfields and the Irwin gardens); ethnic gardens (International Friendship Gardens and Shiojiri Niwa

Friendship Garden); demonstration gardens (The Display Garden, White River Gardens, and Purdue Horticultural Gardens); theme or special collection gardens (Warsaw Biblical Gardens, Richmond Rose Gardens, Clark-Landsbaum Holly Arboretum); sunken gardens (Lakeside Rose Garden, Huntington, West Baden Springs, Garfield Park); botanical gardens (Fernwood, Wellfield, Western Kentucky); conservatories (Potawatomi Park South Bend, Foelinger-Friemann); arboretums (Taltree, Hayes, Indiana University); and pleasure gardens (Ogden Park, Jennie Thompson, Foster Park, Arts Park, Coxhall, and Cathedral gardens).

The guide book is dedicated to those interested in exploring the beauty and botanical richness of Indiana. Many visitors to public gardens will find landscaping ideas to apply at home in their personal gardens for their horticultural enrichment. May this guide inspire many joy-filled, floral memories.

Ravine Garden, Oldfields Estate, Indianapolis Museum of Art

Main Garden Entrance, Ogden Gardens, Valparaiso

Indiana Public Gardens

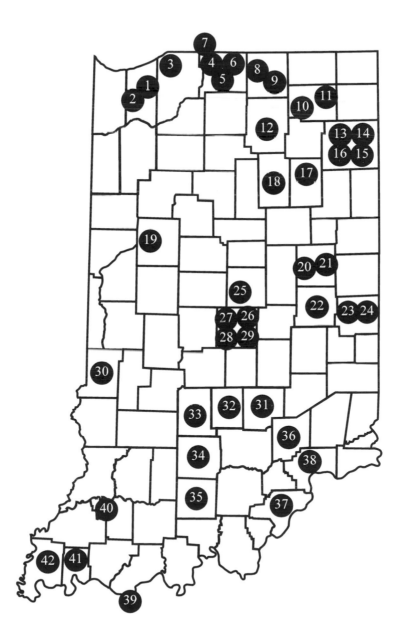

Ogden Gardens

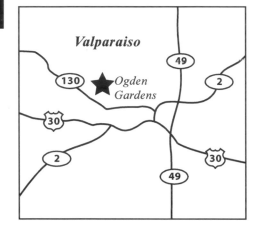

Valparaiso

Ogden Gardens

Harrison Blvd.

Yellowstone St.

Ogden Gardens

Campbell Street

Calumet Avenue

Lincolnway Avenue

Downtown Valparaiso

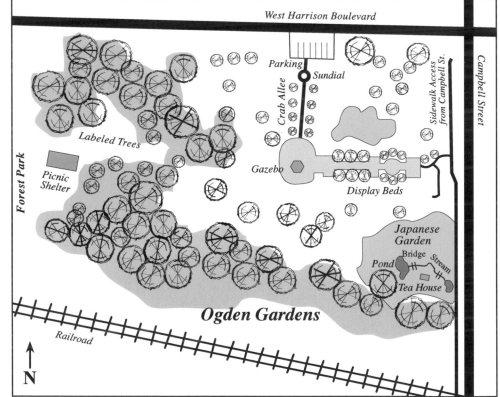

West Harrison Boulevard

Parking

Sundial

Crab Allee

Sidewalk Access from Campbell St.

Campbell Street

Labeled Trees

Forest Park

Picnic Shelter

Gazebo

Display Beds

Japanese Garden

Pond *Bridge* *Stream*

Tea House

Ogden Gardens

Railroad

N

1. OGDEN GARDENS
VALPARAISO, INDIANA

> *"To the attentive eye, each moment of the year has its own beauty."*
>
> **Ralph Waldo Emerson**

Ogden Gardens is a four acre visual delight that is owned and managed by the Valparaiso Department of Parks and Recreation. Development of the gardens began in the 1950s under the supervision of the first park district gardener, Otto Ogden, for whom the garden is named in honor of his dedication and wonderful work.

Winding brick and stone pathways lead beside overflowing, color-filled beds filled with native and exotic annuals, perennials and ornamental grasses. The central plaza and memorial garden area features a gazebo that is a popular spot for social events.

Located at the southeast corner of the gardens is a Japanese Tea Garden. Interconnecting stone pathways lead past a waterfall, a rock-lined stream and a koi-filled pond. Decorative bridges span the waterway to the tea house that overlooks the gardens.

The west garden lawn features shade and flowering trees and shrubs with several benches intermingled throughout for relaxation and contemplation. For ease of identification, a plant list of 125 species is available at the gardens entrance adjacent to the parking area which corresponds with the numbered plant tags located throughout the gardens.

Ogden Gardens is located in residential west central Valparaiso, 0.75 miles north of Lincolnway Avenue/SR 130 at 451 Harrison Boulevard at the intersection of Campbell Street and Harrison Boulevard. A mini parking lot is located on Harrison Boulevard just west of the traffic light.

Additional parking is located west of the gardens in adjoining Forest Park, accessible from Harrison Boulevard. Ten acre Forest Park features open and rolling oak-hickory forest and includes such amenities as two picnic shelters, playfields, a playground, all-weather paths, and restrooms.

*Ogden Gardens, 451 Harrison Blvd., (corner of Campbell St. & Harrison Blvd.), Valparaiso, IN 46385 **Tel:** (219) 531-4678, 462-5144 **Web:** www.valparaisoparks.org **Open:** daily, dawn to dusk **Acreage:** 4 acres **Fee(s):** facility rental **Botanical Collection(s):** display gardens, Japanese garden, native garden, shrubs, trees, grasses.

Japanese Tea House & Koi Pond, Ogden Gardens, Valparaiso

Taltree Arboretum & Gardens

Valparaiso

130

30

Taltree
Arboretum
& Gardens

2

2

30

49

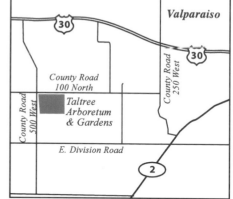

Valparaiso

30

30

County Road
100 North

Taltree
Arboretum
& Gardens

County Road
500 West

County Road
250 West

E. Division Road

2

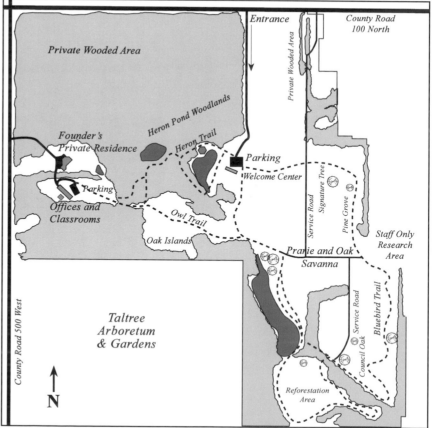

Private Wooded Area

Entrance

County Road
100 North

Private Wooded Area

Heron Pond Woodlands

Heron Trail

*Founder's
Private Residence*

Parking

Welcome Center

Signature Tree

Service Road

Pine Grove

Parking

Offices and
Classrooms

Owl Trail

Oak Islands

*Prairie and Oak
Savanna*

Staff Only
Research
Area

County Road 500 West

Taltree
Arboretum
& Gardens

Council Oak

Service Road

Bluebird Trail

Reforestation
Area

N

2. TALTREE ARBORETUM & GARDENS
VALPARAISO, INDIANA

Established in 1998 by the Gabis Family Foundation, Taltree Arboretum and Gardens is a 300 acre reserve of display gardens, woody plant collections, restored woodlands, savanna, wetlands and prairie. Taltree is dedicated to restoring and preserving the native landscape of northwestern Indiana

There are formal and semi-formal garden areas designed to provide pleasure and education. The Welcome Center Garden is displayed to the immediate north of the welcome center and visitor parking area, and features oriental maples, viburnums, lilacs, conifers, other woody plants and perennials. To the west of the Welcome Center, the Joseph E, Meyer Memorial Pavilion Garden exhibits a rich variety of native plants. The Audrey and Leonard Hitz Family Rose Garden, situated directly south behind the welcome center, includes roses and flowering trees set in a plaza of geometrically arranged limestone blocks. A few yards south of the rose garden, the Native Plant Garden showcases Midwestern perennial plants in a naturalistic setting.

> *"Trees are much like human beings and enjoy each others' company. Only a few love to be alone."*
>
> **Jens Jensen**

The arboretum is especially noted for the oak trees that thrive beyond the cultivated gardens in the adjoining prairie and woodland. A unique feature is the Oak Island Exhibit; a collection of oak species from temperate regions worldwide that are arranged geographically and ecologically. Additional natural areas include savanna, white pine groves, buttonbush swamp, and a pond. There are over three miles of interconnecting walking paths that begin and end at the Welcome Center where a trail map brochure and other information are available.

The Taltree staff conducts an ongoing educational series of naturalist and horticulture programs for youth and adults throughout the year. The Joseph E. Meyer Memorial Pavilion and Classroom are available to rent. The Music in Nature Concert Series and other cultural events take place at the pavilion during the warmer months.

There are two entrances to Taltree. The Visitors Arboretum entrance is located at Porter CR 450 West 100 North and the Administrative and Classroom entrance is located at Porter CR 71 North 500 West.

*Taltree Arboretum & Gardens (10 miles west and south of Valparaiso), 450 West 100 North, Valparaiso, IN 46385 **Tel:** (219) 462-0025 **Web:** www.taltree.org **Open:** daily, 8:00 a.m.-5:00 p.m. CST, Office Hours, M-F, 8:30 a.m.- 4:30 p.m. **Acreage:** 300 **Fee(s):** admission, special events, educational programs, facility rental, guided tours, membership **Botanical Collections:** arboretum, display gardens, rose garden, native plants, oaks.

Oak Savanna,
Taltree Arboretum & Gardens, Valparaiso

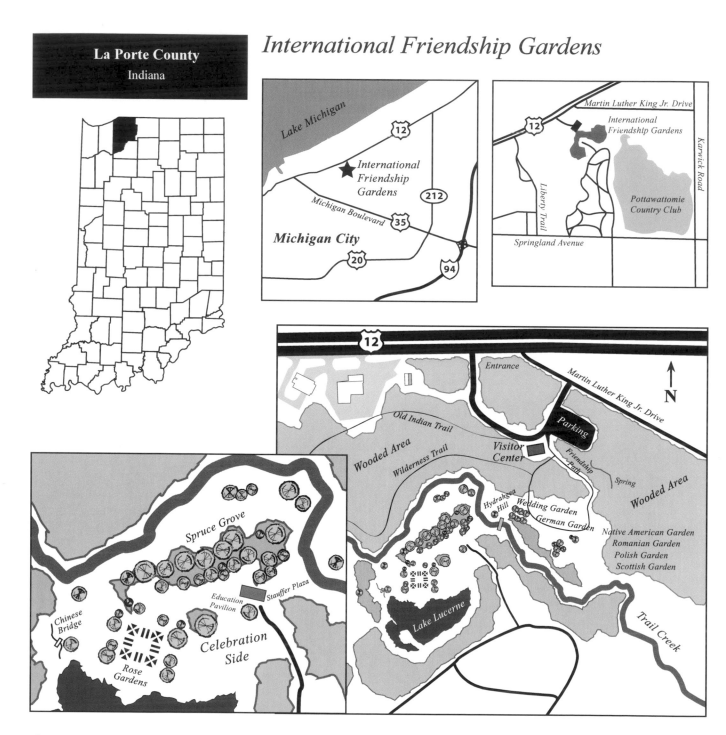

International Friendship Gardens

La Porte County
Indiana

Lake Michigan

International Friendship Gardens

Michigan Boulevard

Michigan City

Martin Luther King Jr. Drive

International Friendship Gardens

Liberty Trail

Pottawattomie Country Club

Springland Avenue

Karwick Road

Entrance

Martin Luther King Jr. Drive

Parking

Old Indian Trail

Wooded Area

Wilderness Trail

Visitor Center

Friendship Path

Spring

Wooded Area

Hydrangea Hill

Wedding Garden

German Garden

Native American Garden
Romanian Garden
Polish Garden
Scottish Garden

Lake Lucerne

Trail Creek

N

Spruce Grove

Education Pavilion

Stauffer Plaza

Chinese Bridge

Celebration Side

Rose Gardens

3. INTERNATIONAL FRIENDSHIP GARDENS
MICHIGAN CITY, INDIANA

Chinese Bridge & Garden,
International Friendship Garden, Michigan City

Peace and friendship to all nations of the world is expressed in the landscape of the International Friendship Gardens. As its place name implies, the International Friendship Gardens botanically represents several countries and ethnics around the world. The noble mission of the philanthropic institution is to promote world friendship through gardening, and to enhance the lives of visitors by artistic, musical and nature-related programs.

Historically, the gardens have a rich and colorful past. After the close of the Chicago's World's Fair, A Century of Progress, in 1934, the modified gardens were re-established in 1936 in the fertile floodplain of Trail Creek, located a mile south of Lake Michigan at Michigan City. Mr. And Mrs. Frank Warren generously offered the Trail Creek site, and the gardens were developed by three Stauffer brothers, nursery men from Hammond, Indiana, who had created the original garden at the World's Fair. Presidents, kings, queens, governors, artists, musicians, educators, scientists and many other world-famous, constituted the charter membership and were responsible for its founding.

During the gardens heyday from 1936-1970, the botanical collections thrived, but later declined due to a lack of interest and shift in cultural values. However, the gardens saw a resurgence beginning in the 1980s thanks to the leadership role of Jean Houck, who organized and led a support group of Friends of the Gardens to stop the garden's decline and save it from extinction. Today, the gardens are maintained by volunteers who are dedicated to returning the gardens to their former grandeur.

> *"We hope the world may become as friendly as flowers in a garden."*
>
> **Clarence Stauffer**

The 106 acres are near-evenly divided between the developed gardens of the Trail Creek valley and the surrounding natural wooded upland dunes that are interlaced with nearly two miles of meandering hiking trails. A map of the trails and gardens is available.

From the parking lot and Visitor's Cabin, the Path of Nations or the Friendship Path descends down the wooded hillside to the gardens along Trail Creek. A bridge spans Trail Creek and leads to Celebration Side.

The ethnic gardens include the Native American, Romanian, Norwegian, Scottish, German, and Polish gardens. Additional gardens and features of interest include Lake Lucerne, a Rose Garden, Symphony Garden, Bog Garden, Hydrangea Hill, Stauffer Memorial and Elston Bell, Stauffer Plaza, Spruce Grove, Chinese Bridge, Peace Bell, Education Pavilion, Lithuanian Monuments, and the Path of Nations Spring.

*International Friendship Gardens, 2500 E. U.S. Hwy 12, P. O. Box 8834, Michigan City, IN 46360-8834 **Tel:** (219) 878-9885 **Web:** www.friendshipgardens.org **Open:** May (Mother's Day weekend) through October, Tuesday-Sunday, 10 a.m.- 4 p.m., also by appt. **Acreage:** 106 **Fee(s):** admission, special events, educational programs, facility rental, membership **Botanical Collections:** ethnic gardens, native forest, varied habitat.

Historic Oliver Gardens

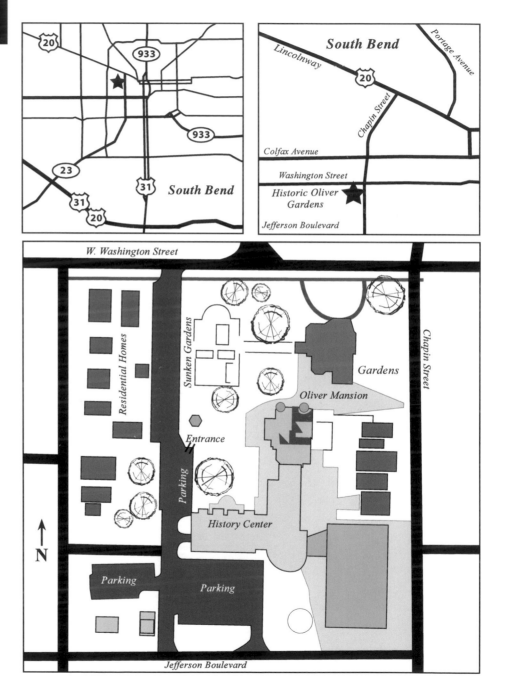

4. HISTORIC OLIVER GARDENS
SOUTH BEND, INDIANA

> *"What does he plant who plants a tree?*
> *The joy that unborn eyes shall see---*
> *And far cast thought of civic good---*
> *His blessings on the neighborhood."*
>
> **Henry C. Bunner**

The Historic Oliver Gardens are located on the 2.5 acre grounds of Copshaholm, the historic estate of Joseph Doty Oliver, former President of the Oliver Chilled Plow Works, and son of Scottish immigrant, James Oliver, inventor of the chilled plow. Copshaholm, a Romanesque Queen Anne-styled house, was completed in 1896 and bears the ancient place name for Newcastleton, Scotland, the home of his father.

Adjacent west of the home is the formal Italianate garden that was designed by interior designer, Alice Neale in 1907, and whose legacy remains largely intact. Components of the garden include brick pathways, multiple levels, geometrically-shaped beds, a tennis lawn, fountain, a long pergola that stretches along the west edge of the lawn, and a tea house.

The gardens reflect a Victorian taste for flowers and include numerous perennials such as daffodils, tulips, peonies, lilies and irises and also woody plants that include lilacs, roses, boxwood and dogwoods. A cut stone wall and wooden fence ensures privacy, shielding the garden from undesirable views of the adjacent street and parking area. The gardens are being restored to appear as they were during the early 20th century when the Oliver family entertained family and friends with lawn socials and tennis parties. The gardens and home are listed on the National Register of Historic Places.

The showiest time to visit the gardens is in May and June. There is no charge to visit the Oliver Gardens; however, visitors may want to explore Copshaholm, the Worker's Home and the Northern Indiana Center for History's exhibit galleries (fee charged). The complex is located west of downtown at the southwest corner of the intersection of Washington and Chapin streets.

*Historic Oliver Gardens, Copshaholm, Northern Indiana Center for History, 808 W. Washington Street, South Bend, IN 46601 **Tel:** (574) 235-9664 **Web:** www.centerforhistory. org **Open:** daily, Sunday 12 p.m.-5 p.m., Monday-Saturday. 10 a.m.-5 p.m. **Acreage:** 2.5 acre grounds, gardens less than one **Fee(s):** special events, programs, facility rental, museums **Botanical Collections:** historic estate garden, Victorian-styled flower garden, Italianate-styled garden.

Italianate Formal Garden, Historic Oliver Gardens, South Bend

Potawatomi Park Conservatories

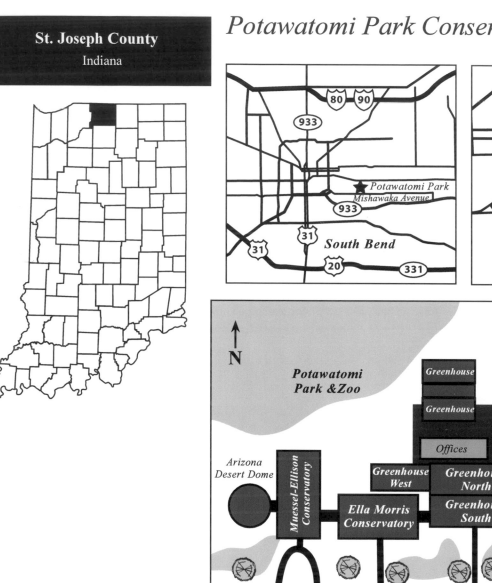

St. Joseph County
Indiana

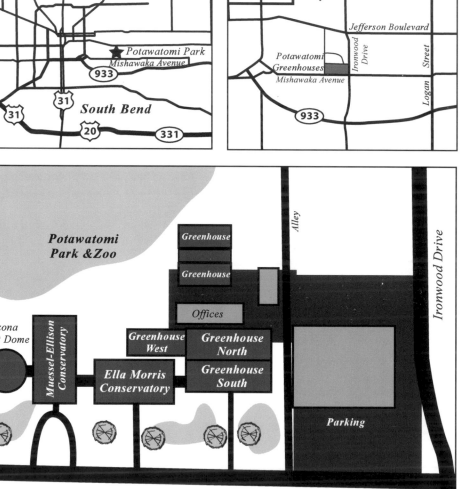

5. POTAWATOMI PARK CONSERVATORIES
SOUTH BEND, INDIANA

> *"He who loves a garden loves a greenhouse too."*
>
> **William Cowper**

Sometimes referred to as the South Bend Conservatories, this city-owned, historic greenhouse complex is situated at the southeast corner of Potawatomi Park which is also home to the city zoo. America's premier greenhouse designer, Lord and Burnham, the same firm that planned conservatories for the U. S. Botanic Garden and the New York Botanical garden, designed most of the South Bend conservatories.

The Potawatomi Greenhouse, built in the 1920s, is actually eight growing glass houses that cultivate thousands of flowers and seasonal plantings for the city parks and public places around South Bend. In addition, the "working" greenhouses cultivate plants for the adjoining conservatories including three lavish seasonal and holiday floral shows.

The three interconnecting conservatories were added to the greenhouses during the 1960s and 1970s. Thanks to the generous funding provided by the Morris, Muessel and Ellison families, two conservatories were constructed in the 1960s. The Ella Morris Conservatory features a rich variety of tropical and sub-tropical flowering plants such as rubber trees, bamboo, and citrus. The Muessel-Ellison Conservatory contains a small waterfall and is filled with flowering exotics including bougainvillea and bird of paradise flowers. The Arizona Desert Dome was added in 1973. Various arid plants such as cacti, succulents and century plants from the Sonoran Desert zone are exhibited in a circular display. The conservatories are popular sites for weddings, school biology study groups, and meeting places for social organizations.

Due to rising costs in recent years, the city of South Bend had planned to close these historic legacies, but concerned citizens and the Botanical Society of South Bend protested the closing and raised monies to secure these botanical treasures.

The conservatories are located southeast of downtown at 2105 Mishawaka Avenue across from the River Park library branch.

Tropical Collection,
Potawatomi Park Conservatories, South Bend

*Potawatomi Park Conservatories**, 2105 Mishawaka Ave., South Bend, IN 46615 **Tel:** (574) 235-9442 **Web:** www.sbpark.org **Open:** daily, Sun. & Sat., 12 p.m.-5:00 p.m., Mon.-Fri. 9 a.m.-5:00 p.m. **Acreage:** 2 **Fee(s):** admission, facility rental, special events, educational programs, plant sales, membership **Botanical Collections:** conservatory exhibits, tropical, subtropical and Sonoran Desert plants.

Shirojiri Niwa Friendship Garden

St. Joseph County
Indiana

South Bend-Mishawaka

80 90

Shirojiri Garden

933

331

31

20

331

Jefferson Boulevard

St. Joseph River

Merrifield Park
East Mishawaka Ave.

933

Lincolnway East

Main Street

Byrkit Avenue

Mishawaka

Merrifield Park

East Mishawaka Ave.

N

Rock Garden

Bridge

Bridge

North Niles Avenue

Merrifield Park

Entrance

Statue

Tea House

North Indiana Avenue

Joseph Street

6. SHIOJIRI NIWA FRIENDSHIP GARDEN
MISHAWAKA, INDIANA

> *"The most basic element of any Japanese garden design comes from the realization that every detail has a significant value."*
>
> *Elizabeth Barber*

Dedicated August 1987, the city-owned Shiojiri Niwa is a 1.3 acre Japanese "strolling garden" (Chiseno-Kaiyushiki) that symbolizes the sister-city relationship between Mishawaka, Indiana and Shiojiri City, Nagano Prefecture, Japan. Designed by Hidekazu Yokozawa, the bronze sculpture at the garden entrance of two American and two Japanese children illustrates the special relationship between the two cities that began in 1964 when elementary school children started a cultural exchange. The garden design was created by landscape architect Shoji Kanaoka. The bridges, teahouse pavilion and entry gate were designed by Phil Cartwright.

Japanese gardens are artfully designed to emphasize the importance of the religious philosophy and symbolic elements of Shintoism and Zen Buddhism. The garden park is traditionally designed as an oasis of peace, thus, instilling a reverence for nature.

Although Shiojiri is a "dry" garden, the element of water is symbolized by raked sand and gravel and "cascading" stone-laden beds. The large boulders represent islands. The five pine tree varieties found in the garden symbolize long life and happiness. The lack of striking vibrant color of flowers and the emphasis of lush greens and browns is intended to achieve calmness; however, some color is added for the element of surprise.

The element of garden accessories such as bridges, buildings, fences, and gates are also important in the Japanese Garden. The Garden Bridge is a symbolic link between earth and heaven, whereas the garden's Zig-Zag Bridge

Spring at Shiojiri Garden, Mishawaka

eludes evil spirits. The physical high point of Shiojiri Niwa is the tea house pavilion, a place to appreciate, contemplate and view the garden. Long term skilled maintenance of the garden will further enhance its simplistic beauty, making it more desirable of the public's attention and admiration.

Shiojiri Niwa, a Mishawaka park facility, is located at 1000 E. Mishawaka Avenue, between Niles Avenue and Indiana Avenue, south and east of Merrifield Park and Pool, and the St. Joseph River in Mishawaka.

*Shiojira Niwa Friendship Garden, 1000 E. Mishawaka Ave., Merrifield Park Complex, Mishawaka, IN 46545
Tel: (574) 258-1664 **Web:** www.mishawakacity.com **Open:** daily, dawn to dusk **Acreage:** 1.3 **Fee(s):** facility rental
Botanical Collections: Japanese strolling garden.

Fernwood Botanical Garden & Nature Preserve

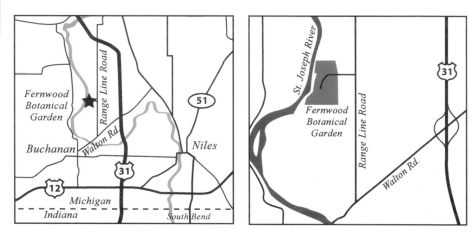

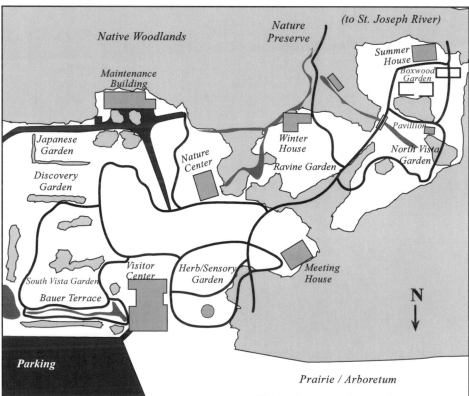

7. FERNWOOD BOTANICAL GARDEN & NATURE PRESERVE
BUCHANAN, MICHIGAN

> *"One of the attractive things about the flowers is their beautiful reserve."*
> **Henry D. Thoreau**

Located in neighboring southwest Michigan, not far north of the state line, Fernwood is situated within the Greater South Bend-Michiana area. Fernwood, a private, non-profit educational center for gardening, nature study and arts and crafts, has been open to the public since 1964. The 105 acre rural countryside treasure borders the St. Joseph River and embraces eight acres of themed gardens and facilities surrounded by 30 acres of native forest preserve that is interlaced with walking paths, an 18 acre wilderness area, and a 45 acre arboretum and reconstructed prairie.

In addition to the visitor center with its tropical conservatory, library, classrooms, art gallery, gift shop, café and terrace, the adjoining grounds feature a nature center, meeting house, winter house, summer house, water wheel, pavilion, dovecote, statuary and benches. The numerous gardens that are clustered about the visitor center and other facilities include the Native Plant Garden, Children's Discovery Garden, Japanese Garden, Hosta Bowl, Ravine Rock Garden, Fern Garden, Wildflower Garden, Boxwood Garden, Lilac Garden, Lily Pond, Cottage Border Garden, and a Herb and Sensory Garden.

The adjacent forest is a dedicated nature preserve that includes a variety of habitats ranging from riparian floodplain forest to an old field succession forest. Various seeps and springs from the upper bluffs spill down to the river below. The five acre reconstructed tall grass prairie and arboretum are located in the open meadow, north of the entry drive and facilities. The Michigan Department of Natural Resources includes Fernwood as one of their designated Wildlife Viewing Areas.

Fernwood relies on volunteers and membership to help maintain the gardens and operate the facilities. A wide variety of educational and cultural programming is scheduled throughout the year.

Located in Berrien County, north of Buchanan, Michigan, Fernwood is reached from South Bend via U.S. 31 highway, exit 7 onto Walton Road, then 1.5 mile west to Range Line Road, then north 1.7 miles to the entrance. Follow the highway signs.

*Fernwood Botanical Garden & Nature Preserve (12 miles NW of South Bend), 1720 Range Line road, Niles, MI 49120 **Tel:** (269) 683-8653, 695-6491 **Web:** www.fernwoodbotanical.org **Open:** Summer - April 1 - Oct. 31, Sunday 12 p.m.- 6 p.m., Tues.- Sat., 10 a.m.- 6 p.m. EDT Winter - Nov. 1- March 31, Sunday 12 p.m.- 5 p.m., Tues.- Sat. 10 a.m.- 5 p.m. EST, closed Mondays, Easter Sunday, Thanksgiving weekend & two weeks during Christmas & New Years **Acreage:** 105 **Fee(s):** admission, facility rental, special events, educational programs, membership **Botanical Collections:** thematic gardens, conservatory, wildflowers, arboretum, prairie, nature preserve.

Dovecote, Herb & Sensory Garden, Fernwood, Buchanan, Michigan

Wellfield Botanic Gardens

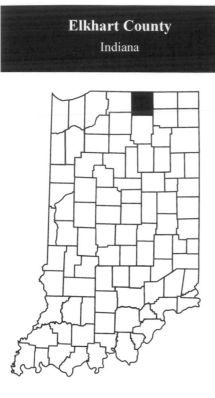

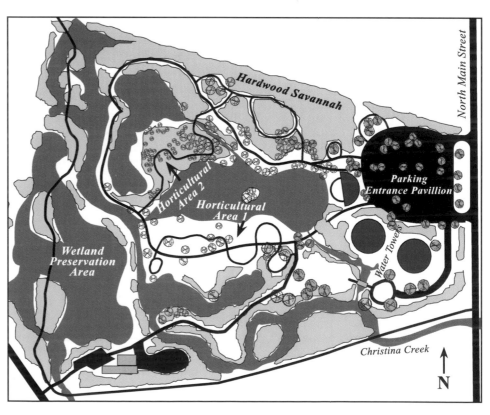

8. WELLFIELD BOTANIC GARDENS
ELKHART, INDIANA

A work in progress, the 36 acre Wellfield Botanic Gardens site has been made possible with a gift from the Elkhart Rotary Club to commemorate the 100th anniversary of Rotary International. The Elkhart Rotary Club funded the conceptual design and Master Plan for the site that is now being operated as a nonprofit corporation. Designed by landscape architects Buettner and Associates of Milwaukee, Wisconsin, they are creating a living work of art that will be developed in seven stages over the next ten years. Phase I was completed in the fall of 2008.

> *"If there is magic on the planet,*
> *it is contained in the water."*
>
> ***Loren Eisley***

Located on the site of the city of Elkhart's main well field, the purpose of the gardens is "connecting mind, body and spirit with nature" with a mission of education about the restoration and conservation of freshwater and its environs. The gardens will create outdoor learning centers and educational programs will focus on wetlands, the hardwood forests, and their relationship to freshwater. Wetlands and ponds comprise nearly half of the acreage and four acres includes a mature oak-hickory forest. Christina Creek forms the west and south boundary of the site. Diverted creek waters replenish the adjacent wetlands and ponds of the gardens.

In time, the botanic site will feature 22 thematic display gardens and event spaces that will include a Water Garden, Waterfall Garden, English Cottage Garden, Wedding Garden, Spring Garden, Sensory Garden, Pergola Garden, Hosta Garden, Children's Garden, Sculpture Garden, Annual Garden, Asian Island Garden, Event Garden, Contemporary Garden, Ceremony Garden, Memorial Garden and Midwest Woodland Garden, all along a half mile promenade. In addition, a Visitor's Center with restaurant/deli, gift shop, event space will be constructed along with the Horticultural Center that will have classroom and greenhouse facilities. Volunteers and donors are welcome to assist in the gardens development.

Overflow Lip,
Wellfield Botanic Garden, Elkhart

*__Wellfield Botanic Gardens__, 1000 N. Main Street, P. O. Box 476, Elkhart, IN 46515-0476 __Tel:__ (574) 266-2006 __Web:__ www.wellfieldgardens.org __Open:__ Summer-6 a.m.-8 p.m., Winter- 8 a.m.- 6 p.m. __Acreage:__ 36 __Fee__(s): none currently, future admission, facility rental, garden membership __Botanical Collections:__ thematic display gardens, wetlands, aquatic plants, native forest.

Krider Nurseries World's Fair Garden

Elkhart County
Indiana

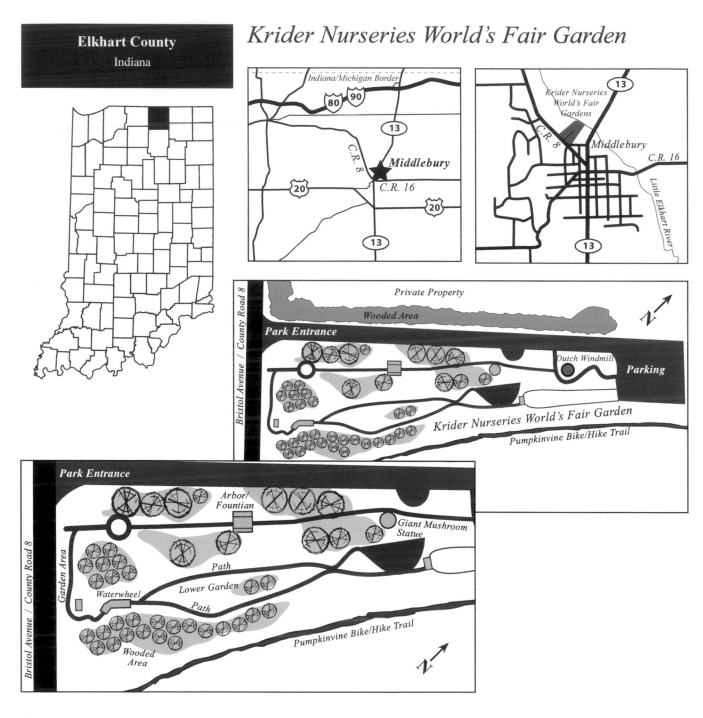

9. KRIDER NURSERIES WORLD'S FAIR GARDEN
MIDDLEBURY, INDIANA

Founded in 1896 by Vernon Krider (1876-1955), Krider Nurseries produced its first catalog in 1906 and for many years, Krider's was one of Middlebury's largest industries. Formerly a schoolteacher, Mr. Krider became a berry fruit farmer and his efforts and interests evolved into the nursery business. Primarily a regional wholesale business, the nursery also served the mail-order market. A unique botanic distinction, Krider bought the patent to produce and sell the first thornless roses.

> *"The nursery at the present time [1931] is the largest and best equipped of any nursery between Cleveland and Chicago."*
>
> **Charles Roll**

Krider Nurseries constructed and exhibited Krider's Diversified Garden at the Century of Progress International Exposition "World's Fair" in Chicago (1933-1934), an investment of $10,000. Krider created a series of landscape dioramas embellished with plant materials including a miniature mill house with working water wheel, a Dutch windmill and Mushroom Tea House. The gardens were a successful promotion for Krider Nurseries and its mail order business.

Some plants and structures were returned to Middlebury after the closing of the Chicago Exposition, and the "dream garden" was reconstructed in 1935. After years of being Middlebury's most successful enterprise, Krider's Nurseries ceased operation in 1990 and the gardens fell into decay. Realizing the historic value of the gardens, they were restored by the community in 1995 and are now a community park.

Today's visitors may stroll along the shaded landscaped loop with its waterfalls, fountains, reflecting pools and lily pond, and picnic, relax and enjoy Krider's historic "dream" gardens. The Greenway Pumpkinvine Nature Trail travels alongside the east border of the gardens.

The garden park is located in the community of Middlebury in northeastern Elkhart County at 302 W. Bristol Street/C.R. 18, across from the local historical society museum and just west of the fire station. A roadside Indiana state historical marker is located near the entrance.

*Krider's Nurseries "World's Fair" Gardens**, 302 W. Bristol St./C.R. 18, Middlebury, IN 46540 **Tel**: (574) 825-1499 **Web**: www.middleburyin.com **Open**: daily, dawn to dusk **Acreage**: 2.4 **Fee(s)**: facility rental **Botanical Collections**: display gardens, annuals, perennials, historic World's Fair Garden.

Giant Toadstool,
Krider Nurseries World's Fair Garden, Middlebury

Noble County
Indiana

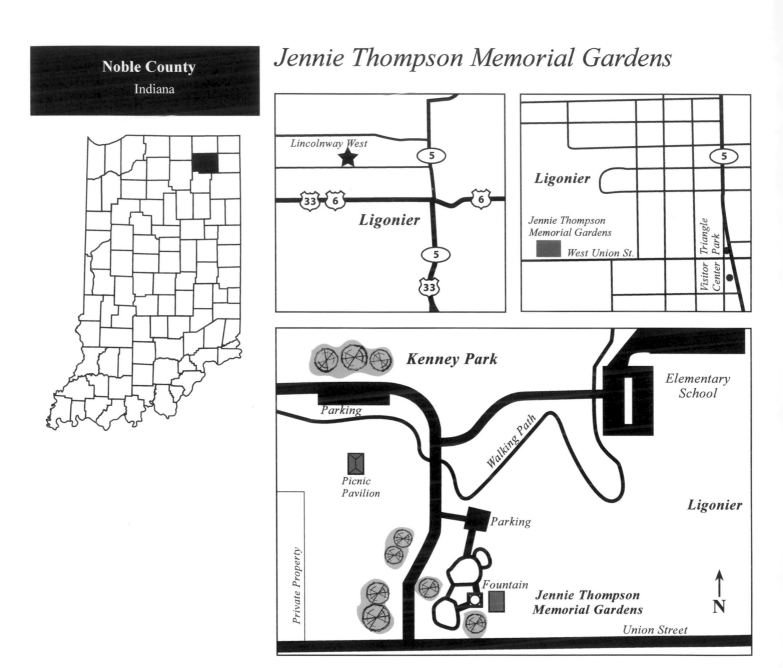

Lincolnway West

5

33 6   6

Ligonier

5

33

Ligonier

5

Jennie Thompson
Memorial Gardens

West Union St.

Visitor Triangle
Center Park

Kenney Park

Elementary
School

Parking

Walking Path

Picnic
Pavilion

Parking

Ligonier

Fountain

**Jennie Thompson
Memorial Gardens**

Private Property

Union Street

N

10. JENNIE THOMPSON MEMORIAL GARDENS
LIGONIER, INDIANA

The one acre Jennie Thompson Memorial Gardens was established in 1993 at the entrance of Kenney Park, the city of Ligonier's main park. The luxurious floral display gardens are planted with a splendid variety of 12,000 annuals, a delightful welcome to visitors of Kenney Park. A living memorial, the gardens are named in honor of Jennie Thompson (1888-1978), a local benefactor, who as the last of her family line formed a foundation with the proceeds from her estate to improve the quality of life in the Ligonier community.

> *"The flowers are nature's jewels, with whose wealth she decks her summer beauty."*
>
> **George Croly**

Planted the third Saturday in May, the 25 brilliant floral beds radiate out and around the central stone fountain and waterfall. Brick pathways provide up close foot access to the color-filled lavish beds. Benches located beneath dense shade trees provide resting places to sit and admire the striking setting. The showiest time to visit is from June to September. The surrounding grassy park landscape allows plenty of room to expand the gardens at a future time. Picnicking and restroom facilities are also available in the 40 acre Kenney Park.

To reach the Jennie Thompson Memorial Gardens in Ligonier, Indiana, Noble County, take S.R. 5/Lincolnway north from the U.S. 6 intersection to Union Street and turn left or west, then drive past the Indiana Historic Radio Museum and Visitor Center, just south of Wood Triangle Park and Landmark Clock and Garden. Continue on West Union Street to the Kenney Park entrance and the gardens. A parking area is available adjacent north of the gardens.

*Jennie Thompson Memorial Gardens, West Union Street, Ligonier, IN 46767 **Tel:** (260) 894-7344 **Web:** www.ligonierindianachamber.org **Open:** daily, dawn to dusk **Fee(s):** facility rental **Acreage:** 1 **Botanical Collections:** formal flower gardens, annuals, perennials, shade trees.

Inviting Garden Entry,
Jennie Thompson Memorial Gardens, Ligonier

Gene Stratton-Porter Gardens

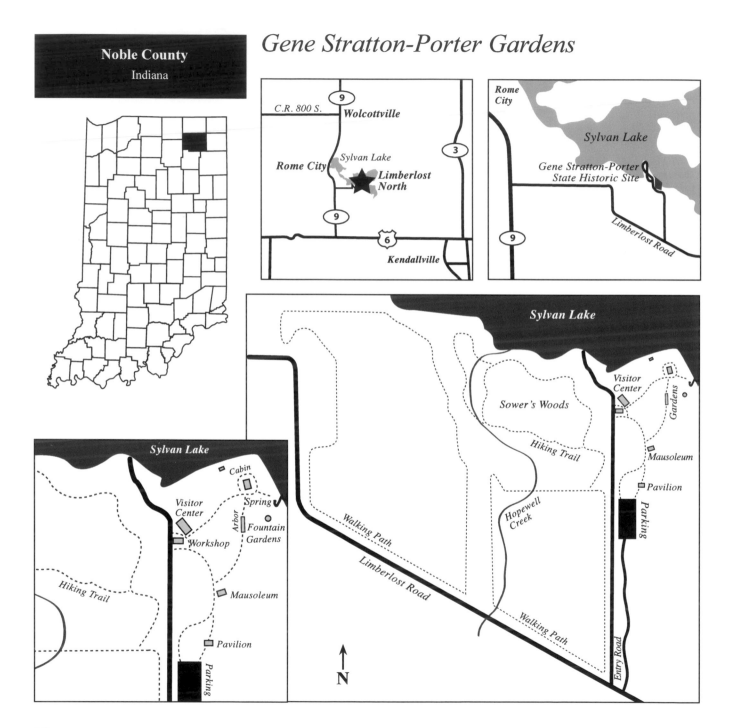

11. GENE STRATTON-PORTER GARDENS & GROUNDS
ROME CITY, INDIANA

Although authoress, naturalist, illustrator and photographer Gene Stratton-Porter's (1864-1924) main subject of her writings, drawings and pictures was the wilds of Indiana, she also loved her domestic cultivated gardens. The restored gardens of Wildflower Woods are located to the immediate south of the Sylvan Lake family cabin (built 1913) bordering the deep shade of "Wildflower Woods," where many endangered native flowers were transplanted by Mrs. Porter from around the state during the early 1900s.

> *"The chief joy of a garden lies in making things live, making them grow abundantly and flower beautifully."*
>
> **Gene Stratton-Porter**

Walking north from the parking and picnic area to the cabin, visitors will pass through the aging deciduous forest, past Mrs. Porter's and her daughter, Jeannette's mausoleum where they are buried beneath their favorite oak tree, to enter the orchard and formal gardens. The gardens are laced with gentle paths that weave among the harmonious mix of flowers, herbs and fruit trees. The extensive long log arbor of wisteria is flanked on both sides by a rich variety of Mrs. Porter's favorite wild and cultivated flowers. There are log benches to rest and study the surroundings, a flowing fountain and Singing Waters Pond. Just east of the gardens, a short path leads to a spring located along the shoreline of Sylvan Lake. There is a posted printed listing and map of the 350 plants growing in the garden. Financial assistance for the formal gardens is provided by the Gene Stratton-Porter Memorial Society. This horticultural treasure is listed in the National Gardens of America Register.

Visitors are welcome to explore on foot the 123 acres of adjoining woods. A hiking trail loops about Sowers Woods and Hopewell Creek to the west of the cabin and gardens. Guided cabin tours are available at regular intervals daily except Monday and the Carriage House Visitors Center features a gift shop. Additional amenities include picnicking, and special events.

*Gene Stratton-Porter State Historic Site, Limberlost North, 1205 Pleasant Point, Box 639, Rome City, IN 46784 **Tel:** (260) 854-3790 **Web:** www.gene-stratton-porter.com **Open:** daily, home tours at regular intervals, grounds open dawn to dusk, cabin and visitors center closed Monday, hours Tues.-Sat. 9 a.m.-5 p.m., Sun. 1 p.m.-5 p.m., cabin tours end one hour earlier **Acreage:** 1 acre gardens, 123 total **Fee(s)** admission, facility rental, Friends membership **Botanical Collections:** historic flower gardens, orchard, native wildflowers, deciduous forest.

Midsummer Garden,
Gene Stratton-Porter Gardens, Rome City

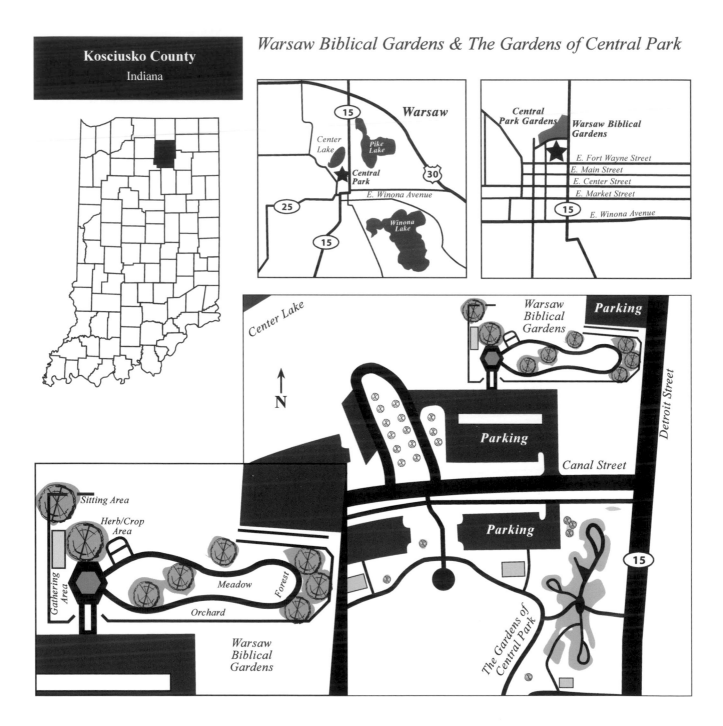

Kosciusko County
Indiana

Warsaw Biblical Gardens & The Gardens of Central Park

Warsaw

15

Center
Lake

Pike
Lake

Central
Park

30

25

15

E. Winona Avenue

Winona
Lake

Central
Park Gardens

Warsaw Biblical
Gardens

E. Fort Wayne Street
E. Main Street
E. Center Street
E. Market Street

15

E. Winona Avenue

Center Lake

N

Warsaw
Biblical
Gardens

Parking

Parking

Canal Street

Parking

Detroit Street

15

The Gardens of Central Park

Sitting Area

Herb/Crop
Area

Gathering Area

Meadow

Forest

Orchard

Warsaw
Biblical
Gardens

12. Warsaw Biblical Gardens & The Gardens of Central Park
Warsaw, Indiana

Officially opening in 1991, the Warsaw Biblical Gardens has become one of the finest religious-themed botanical gardens in the United States. The 0.75 acre garden features over 100 Biblical-identified plants along the 0.25 mile paved walkway loop. A great effort has been brought forth to achieve historical and botanical accuracy of these living floral ties of Judeo-Christian scriptural heritage. The mission of the gardens is

> *"The earth brought forth vegetation, every kind of seed-bearing plant and all kinds of trees that bear fruit containing their seed. God saw that it was good."*
>
> **Genesis 1:12**

to provide, "a rare oasis, rich in beauty and tranquility, a garden accessible for persons of all ages and of all faiths, a botanical resource center for the study of plants of the Bible and an informative, educational and inspirational source."

The Gardens of Central Park, Warsaw

The gardens are divided into six theme or habitat areas mentioned in the Bible: Meadow (flowers), Brook (aquatic plants), Orchard (fruits, grape arbor), Forest (shade trees), Desert (arid plants), and Herbs and Crops (40 varieties). Walk alongside flowering "mallows" or hollyhocks (Job 30:4), marvel at the lovely blooms of "rose" or oleander (Ecclesiastes 39:13), find cool comfort beneath the shade of the "plane" tree or sycamore (Isaiah 50:13), and discover that the "rose" of Sharon is actually a tulip (Song of Solomon 2:1). Non-native and non-hardy plants indigenous to the Middle East are wintered over in greenhouses. Spring and early summer are the best seasons for radiant color. Guided tours and special events are offered from May through September.

Less than 100 yards south across the parking lot and East Canal Street is The Gardens of Central Park, another Warsaw city park featuring botanic amenities. Cobblestone pathways divide the numerous perennial and annual display beds. A striking mix of over 160 varieties of flowers, shrubs and grasses provide a lavish seasonal display. The plants are identified by group label at each bed. A small pond is located at the garden's center. Benches have been provided for relaxation and enjoyment of the gardens.

Both parks are open dawn to dusk April through October. The botanic gardens are located north of downtown Warsaw near the southeast shore of Center Lake, along the north and south sides of East Canal Street, adjacent west of Detroit Street/S.R. 15.

*Warsaw Biblical Gardens & The Gardens of Central Park, 117 E. Canal St., Warsaw, IN 46580 **Tel:** WPD (574) 372-9554, WBG 267-6419, 2692136, GCP 267-1901 **Web:** www.warsawbiblicalgardens.org, www.warsawcity.net **Open:** April 15 through Oct. 15, dawn to dusk **Acreage:** WBG 0.75 acres, GCP 0.33 acres **Fee(s):** WBG donations accepted, facility rental, guided tours, classes, special events, garden membership **Botanical Collections:** Biblical gardens, perennials, annuals.

Meadow, Warsaw Biblical Gardens

The Display Gardens

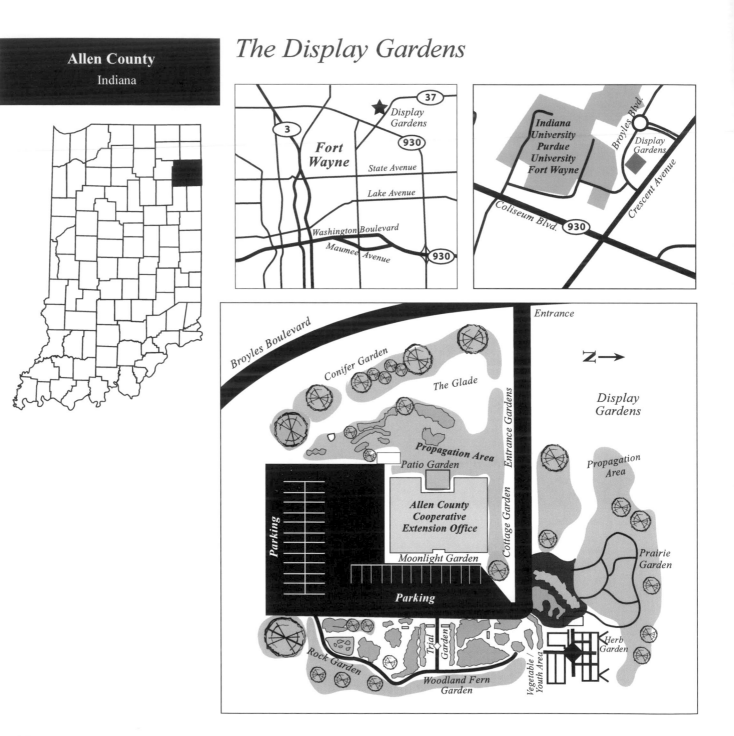

Allen County

Indiana

37

Display
Gardens

3

**Fort
Wayne**

930

State Avenue

Lake Avenue

Washington Boulevard

Maumee Avenue

930

Indiana
University
Purdue
University
Fort Wayne

Broyles Blvd.

Display
Gardens

Coliseum Blvd.

930

Crescent Avenue

Broyles Boulevard

Entrance

Conifer Garden

The Glade

Display
Gardens

Propagation Area

Patio Garden

Propagation
Area

Entrance Gardens

Cottage Garden

**Allen County
Cooperative
Extension Office**

Parking

Moonlight Garden

Prairie
Garden

Parking

Rock Garden

Trial
Garden

Woodland Fern
Garden

Vegetable /
Youth Area

Herb
Garden

13. THE DISPLAY GARDENS
FORT WAYNE, INDIANA

Established in 1989, The Display Gardens were laid out by the Master Gardeners of Allen County who took the initiative to landscape and transform the stark and barren area around the county extension office into a kaleidoscope of horticultural diversity. Demonstration vegetable and flower gardens were first implemented. The next year an outdoor classroom area was added. Throughout the 1990s, the Master Gardeners continued to add a variety of gardens including a Perennial Garden, a Blue and Silver Garden, Woodland Garden and Fairytale Garden. A Garden Open House was held annually and garden plant sales, workshops and garden tours were highly successful.

> *"A garden is a delight to the eye and a solace for the soul."*
>
> ***Sadi***

Since 1998, new gardens have been added and existing gardens have been renovated. Today there are 19 demonstration or "learning" gardens, making The Display Gardens a rewarding place to visit.

A walk through is a delight and an education. The Display Gardens include the Entrance Garden, Birds, Bees & Butterflies Garden, Cottage Garden, Pastel Pathway, Shakespeare Garden, Ornamental Grass Garden, Terrace-Hydrangea Garden, Patio Garden, The Glade, Conifer Garden, Woodland Fen Garden, Japanese Rock Garden, Trial Garden, Everlasting Cutting Garden, Vegetable Youth Garden, Herb Garden, Rock Xeriscape Garden, and Prairie Garden. All of the gardens are funded, designed, planted and maintained by dedicated Master Gardener volunteers for the purpose of sharing gardening information for the public benefit, knowledge and enjoyment.

*The Display Gardens, (located east of IUPFW) Allen County Extension Service, 4001 Crescent Ave., Fort Wayne, IN 46815-4590 Tel: (260) 481-6826 Web: www.extension.purdue.edu/allen Open: daily, dawn to dusk Acreage: 2 Fee(s): none Botanical Collections: demonstration & thematic gardens.

Herb Garden, The Display Gardens, Fort Wayne

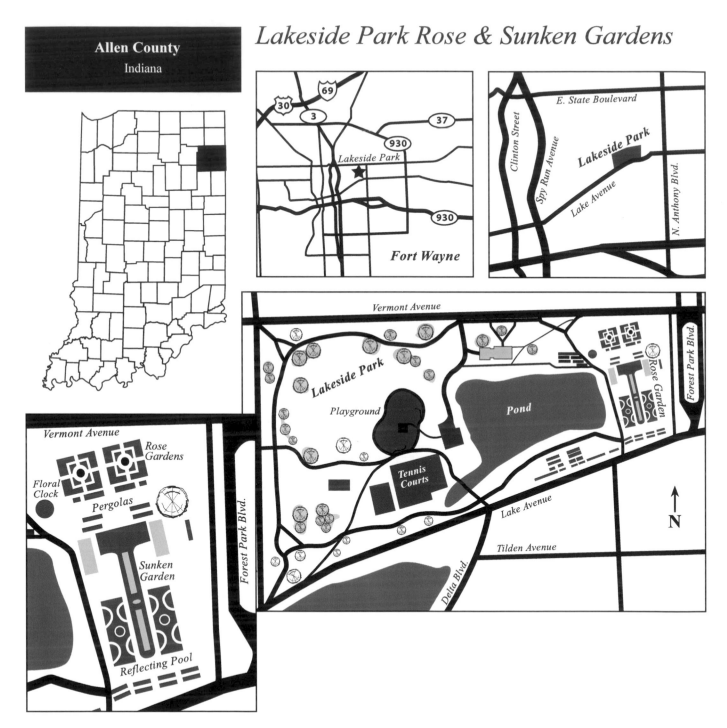

Lakeside Park Rose & Sunken Gardens

Allen County
Indiana

Lakeside Park
Fort Wayne

E. State Boulevard
Clinton Street
Spy Run Avenue
Lakeside Park
Lake Avenue
N. Anthony Blvd.

Vermont Avenue
Lakeside Park
Playground
Pond
Rose Garden
Forest Park Blvd.
Tennis Courts
Lake Avenue
Tilden Avenue
Delta Blvd.
N

Vermont Avenue
Rose Gardens
Floral Clock
Pergolas
Sunken Garden
Reflecting Pool
Forest Park Blvd.

14. LAKESIDE PARK ROSE & SUNKEN GARDENS
FORT WAYNE, INDIANA

Located within the 24 acre Lakeside Park is the three acre Lakeside Rose and Sunken Gardens. Under the supervision of Fort Wayne Parks Superintendent, Adolf Jaenicke (1917-1948), "The City Beautifier," the original gardens were created from a neighborhood trash dump in 1920, and the adjacent rose garden overlooking the lower level formal gardens was completed in the early 1920s. Lakeside was named a National Rose Garden in 1928.

> "O Spirit of the Summertime! Bring back the roses to the dells."
>
> **William Allingham**

Reconstruction of the sunken gardens began in 2005 and was completed a year later at a total cost of over half a million dollars. The pergolas, trellises, reflecting pools, lion's head fountain, retaining walls, stairs, sidewalks and paths were replaced and matched to the original design.

Today's Rose Garden is declared an All-American Rose Selection Public Garden, one of two in Indiana. Lakeside is the largest public rose garden in Indiana and one of the largest in the Midwest. There are over 1,500 roses with over 150 old fashioned and contemporary varieties that bloom in waves of color over the warm months. The rose garden may be rented for an event and is especially popular for weddings. When viewed en masse in June through September, it is understandable why the rose was selected as the national flower of the United States. Additional amenities of Lakeside Park include a floral sun dial, a pond, picnic pavilion, playgrounds, tennis courts and a walking path.

Lakeside Park is located on the near northeast side in a residential neighborhood at 1401 Lake Avenue and Vermont, a few blocks north of the Maumee River and a few blocks east of the St. Joseph River. Street side parking is available along the north edge of the park.

Lakeside Rose Gardens, Fort Wayne

*****Lakeside Park Rose & Sunken Garden,** 1401 Lake Avenue and Vermont, Fort Wayne, IN 46805 **Tel:** (260) 427-6000 **Web:** www.fortwayneparks.org **Open:** daily, dawn to dusk **Acreage:** 3.2 gardens, 24 park total **Fee(s):** facility rental **Botanical Collections:** sunken gardens, formal rose gardens, annuals, perennials, floral sun dial.

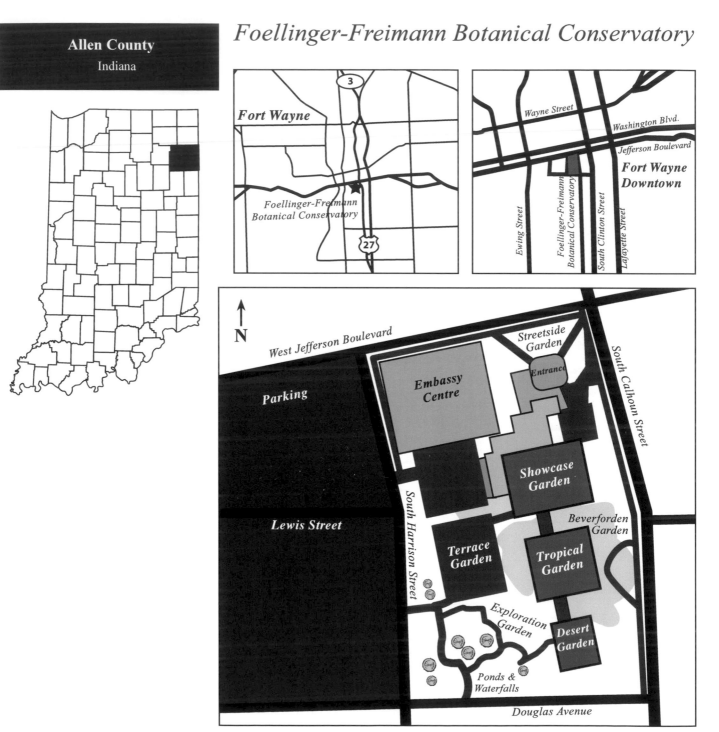

Allen County
Indiana

Foellinger-Freimann Botanical Conservatory

Fort Wayne

3

Foellinger-Freimann
Botanical Conservatory

27

Wayne Street
Washington Blvd.
Jefferson Boulevard

Fort Wayne
Downtown

Ewing Street
Foellinger-Freimann
Botanical Conservatory
South Clinton Street
Lafayette Street

N

West Jefferson Boulevard

Streetside
Garden

Parking

Embassy
Centre

Entrance

South Calhoun Street

Lewis Street

South Harrison Street

Showcase
Garden

Beverforden
Garden

Terrace
Garden

Tropical
Garden

Exploration
Garden

Desert
Garden

Ponds &
Waterfalls

Douglas Avenue

15. Foellinger-Freimann Botanical Conservatory
Fort Wayne, Indiana

Located in the heart of uptown Fort Wayne, the Foellinger-Freimann Botanical Conservatory is one of the largest passive solar conservatories in the Midwest. The building and gardens occupy two city blocks and including the outdoor gardens, total 4.7 acres. The botanic oasis opened in 1983 and is operated and maintained by the Fort Wayne Parks and Recreation Department.

The conservatory consists of three distinct gardens encompassing 24,500 square feet to house over 4,000 plants and 800 species and varieties. The plants are labeled with the common and scientific names, family, native origin, and human usage.

The 10,000 square foot Showcase Garden features four themed seasonal displays annually. Large flowering specimens of angel's trumpet, southern magnolia and loquat thrive year round. The Tropical Garden occupies 10,000 square feet and has

Seasonal Showcase Garden, Foellinger-Freimann Botanical Conservatory, Fort Wayne

the highest point in the glasshouses at 50 feet. Tropical species include orchids, bromeliads, breadfruit, cycads, bird of paradise, tree ferns, dwarf banana, and coffee, orange and chocolate trees. A cascading waterfall and stream flow through the tropical rain forest. Gregarious groups of Japanese white-eye songbirds may be seen or heard in the canopy of the rain forest garden. The 4,500 square foot Desert Garden exhibits plants indigenous to the Sonoran Desert of southern Arizona. The plant life includes creosote bush, century plant, saguaro cactus, fishhook barrel cactus, prickly pear cactus, hairy yucca, ocotillo, ironwood and jojoba shrub.

The outdoor gardens that surround the conservatory includes the Streetside Garden at the main entrance which features ornamental grasses and conifers; the Beverforden Garden at Calhoun and Lewis streets exhibits rhododendrons and other acid soil plants; and the Terrace and Exploration Gardens situated along Douglas Avenue and Harrison Street includes trees, shrubs and perennials.

> *"Whoever loves and understands a garden will find contentment within."*
>
> **Chinese Proverb**

Additional attractions and facilities include the hands-on exhibits in the Discovery Gallery, The Marketplace and The Underground, the Tulip Tree Gift Shop, and several meetings rooms. Special exhibits, events and educational and cultural programs take place throughout the year.

*Foellinger-Freimann Botanical Conservatory**, 1100 S. Calhoun St., Fort Wayne, IN 46802 **Tel:** (260) 427-6440 **Web:** www.botanicalconservatory.org **Open:** Sunday, 12 p.m.- 4 p.m., Tues.-Sat. 10 a.m.-5 p.m., Thurs. open to 8 p.m., closed Mondays, Christmas Day & New Year's Day **Acreage:** 24,500 sq. ft. conservatory, 4.7 acres total **Fee(s):** admission, facility rental, group tours, special events, concert series, art exhibits, lectures, educational programs, horticultural events, plant sales, summer day camp, membership **Botanical Collections:** conservatory, tropical, subtropical, Sonoran Desert, seasonal displays, rhododendrons, conifers, ornamental grasses.

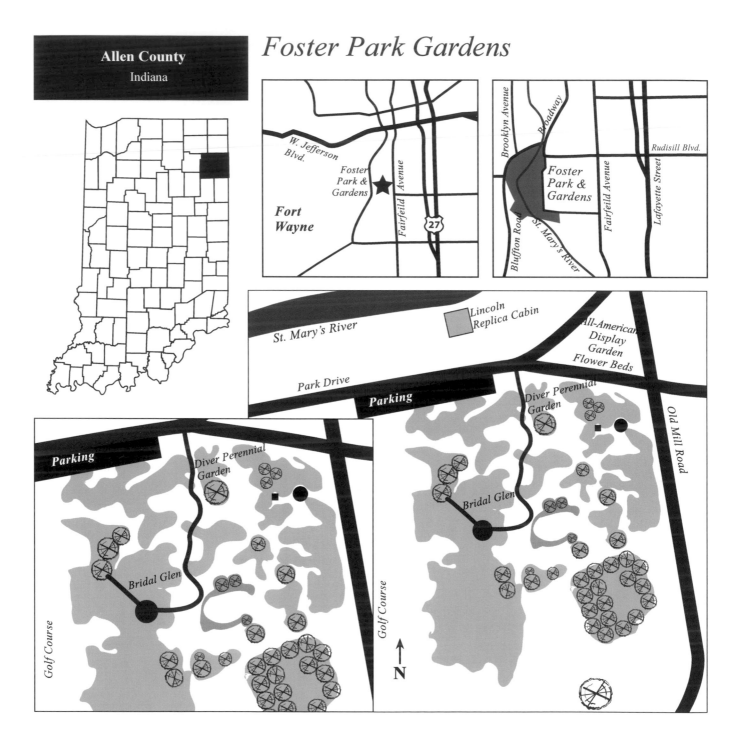

Foster Park Gardens

Allen County
Indiana

W. Jefferson Blvd.

Foster Park & Gardens

Fort Wayne

Fairfeild Avenue

27

Brooklyn Avenue

Broadway

Rudisill Blvd.

Foster Park & Gardens

Fairfeild Avenue

Lafayette Street

Bluffton Road

St. Mary's River

St. Mary's River

Lincoln Replica Cabin

All-American Display Garden Flower Beds

Park Drive

Parking

Diver Perennial Garden

Old Mill Road

Parking

Diver Perennial Garden

Bridal Glen

Golf Course

Bridal Glen

Diver Perennial Garden

Golf Course

N

16. FOSTER PARK GARDENS
FORT WAYNE, INDIANA

> *"The groves were God's first temples."*
>
> **William Cullen Bryant**

Foster Park had its beginnings in 1912, when Samuel and David Foster, the "Fathers of Fort Wayne's Parks," donated the first land tract as a gift to the city of Fort Wayne. Today, Foster Park encompasses 277 acres along four miles of the St. Marys River, south of downtown. The botanical gardens are located near the east Park Drive entrance at the intersection of Broadway and Rudisill Boulevard where parking is available adjacent to the park road.

Featured at Foster Gardens are 32 flower beds planted with 15,000 annual flowers, the All America Selection Display Garden, the Diver Perennial Garden with many unusual perennials, the Robert Glenn Daylily Garden and Bridal Glen with its delicate, heart-shaped trellis, gazebo and arches. Many spring-flowering trees and over 20,000 bulbs open the growing season with spectacular color.

The north portion of Foster Gardens is positioned along the north side of Park Drive overlooking the St. Marys River. Numerous display beds of flowering annuals and perennials surround the replica of Abraham Lincoln's boyhood cabin.

South of the riverside portion of the gardens and Park Drive is the more intimate and private Bridal Glen, the Diver Perennial Garden, the Robert Glenn Daylily Garden and Mead's Garden. Arbors, fountains, a gazebo, stone walls, and benches are elements that enhance the beauty and enjoyment of the floral displays. The large shade trees add charm to the gracious and richly aesthetic level setting that blends naturally with the adjoining golf course. As the name implies, the Bridal Glen is a popular setting for weddings. Additional park amenities include sheltered picnicking, golf course, tennis courts and the Rivergreenway Trail.

Floral Splendor,
Foster Park Gardens, Fort Wayne

*Foster Park Gardens, 3900 Old Mill Road & Rudisill Blvd., Fort Wayne, IN 46805 **Tel:** (260) 427-6000 **Web:** www.fortwayneparks.org **Open:** daily, dawn to dusk **Acreage:** 4 gardens, 277 park total **Fee(s):** facility rental, golf course fees **Botanical Collections:** display beds, perennial garden, Bridal Glen, specimen trees.

Huntington Sunken Garden

Huntington County
Indiana

Clear Creek Rd.

9

5

24

Huntington

Meridian Road

24

224

5

Bartlett Street

Hitzfield St.

Memorial Park

Diamond St.

Sunken Garden

Park Drive

N

Gardens

Bartlett Street

Hitzfield Street

Memorial Park

Diamond Street

Homes

Sunken Gardens

Parking

Park Drive

Parking

Arborial Garden

Homes

Waltonian Garden

Pond

Bartlett Street

Sunken Gardens

Weeping Plant Garden

Pavillion

Park Sign

Tunnel

Park Drive

17.   HUNTINGTON SUNKEN GARDENS
HUNTINGTON, INDIANA

Around 1920, the Keefer & Bailey Lime, Brick, Tile and Cement Company abandoned a lime quarry located at the southwest edge of Huntington, "The Lime City." Seeing the opportunity to create a sunken garden, the city fathers reclaimed the hollowed remains of the lime quarry and transformed it into a horticultural showpiece.

> *"The art of landscaping is that of a fleeting thought that must be caught on the wing."*
>
> **Jens Jensen**

The Chicago Landscape Company created a landscape plan of naturalistic and informal settings with stone stairways leading into the bowl-shaped gardens, field stone footbridges, a horseshoe-shaped pond and amphitheater. Dedicated in 1924, Sunken Gardens became an important feature of the 48 acre Memorial Park. In 1929, the unique garden was featured in the November issue of *Better Homes & Gardens* magazine. Sunken Gardens was a popular destination in its early years, but underwent a decline after World War II.

The historic park was revitalized in the mid-1960s and today, is the showpiece botanic site in the Huntington city park system. It is a popular site of weddings and social events and there is an annual Christmas light display of 80,000 bulbs. The Shakespearian Garden exhibits Elizabethan plants mentioned in the poems and plays of English poet and dramatist William Shakespeare (1564-1616) such as iris, borage, lavender, sage, rosemary and thyme. In addition, Sunken Gardens contain such elements as fountains, a gazebo and picnic tables situated beneath shade trees.

The Waltonian Garden and Arborial Garden, located at the near north end of Memorial Park along Bartlett Street, is just a short walk away from Sunken Gardens. Fountains, ponds, roses, decorative shrubs and flowers surround the gardens that were developed from original plans from the 1920s.

Sunken Gardens is located east of the U.S. 24 and Indiana S.R. 9 intersection. Continue east from the intersection on West Park Drive about a mile to the city park office and the parking area on the south side of the road. The park is bordered by West Park Drive, Dimond, Orchard Hill and Bartlett streets.

Spring at Huntington Sunken Gardens, Huntington

*Huntington Sunken Gardens, 1205 West Park Drive & Dimond Street, Huntington, IN 46750 **Tel:** (260) 358-2323 **Web:** www.huntington.in.us/City/Parks/ **Open:** daily, dawn to dusk **Acreage:** 3 acre garden, 48 park total **Fee(s):** facility rental **Botanical Collections:** sunken gardens, Shakespearian Garden.

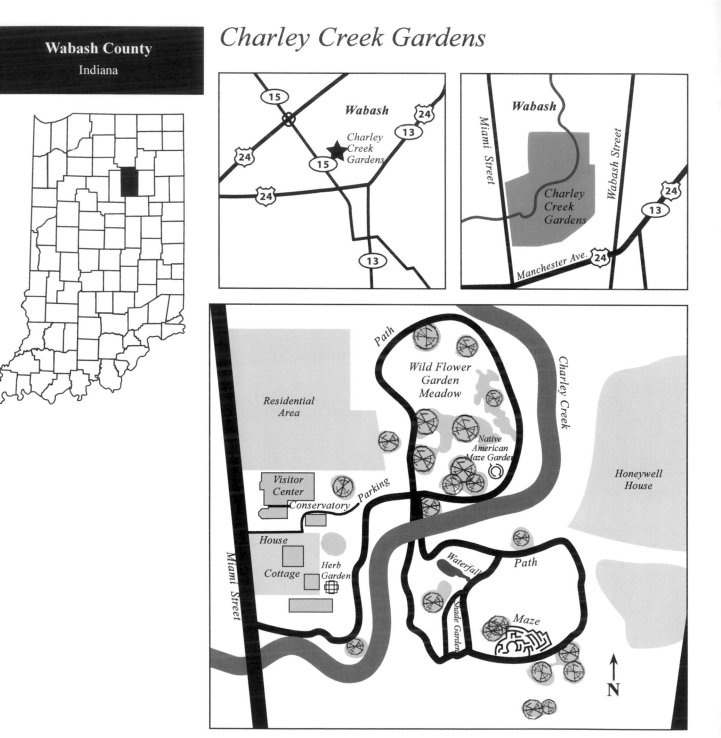

Charley Creek Gardens

Wabash County
Indiana

Wabash

Charley Creek Gardens

Wabash

Miami Street

Charley Creek Gardens

Wabash Street

Manchester Ave.

Path

Wild Flower Garden Meadow

Charley Creek

Residential Area

Native American Maze Garden

Honeywell House

Visitor Center

Parking

Conservatory

House

Waterfall

Path

Cottage

Herb Garden

Shade Garden

Maze

Miami Street

N

18. CHARLEY CREEK GARDENS
WABASH, INDIANA

> *"The man who has planted a garden feels that he has done something for the good of the world."*
>
> **Vita Sackville-West**

Located a few blocks north of downtown Wabash, Charley Creek Gardens is a horticultural center dedicated to the study, conservation and appreciation of plants, both native and exotic, through garden displays, education and research.

Having visited gardens throughout the world, Wabash native, Richard E. Ford, was inspired to create a charming green retreat where area residents and visitors could go for a relaxed day's outing. With the assistance of Charley Creek Foundation, a non-profit group dedicated to historic preservation, the arts and education, Charley Creek Gardens was established.

The garden's Education and Resource Center serves as the central hub of the gardens and is designed in the Arts and Crafts tradition. It includes a resource room, greenhouse, gift shop and restrooms, and houses the horticultural staff offices.

To the east rear of the center and parking area, gravel foot paths lead to the lower creek side floral exhibits. An impressive array of native Indiana plants appears in the lush wildflower floodplain meadow. Nearby is a labyrinth patterned after a Native American Indian design. Further south alongside Charley Creek is the Charley Creek Cottage where ornamental planting about the cottage dazzle the eye and raised beds harbor a variety of herbs and flowers.

Spanning Charley Creek, a decorative foot bridge leads to a bluff-side waterfall that is framed with spring blooming azaleas. Near the base of the 30 foot waterfall is a Bog Garden brimming with plant life native to Indiana wetlands such as marsh marigolds, skunk cabbage and wild iris.

The path continues through the Shade Garden above the meandering creek, providing dazzling seasonal change. Beginning in spring and later in summer, blooming annuals and perennials provide continuous color until autumn when late blooming asters, sunflowers and foliage color provide visual pleasure.

From the Shade Garden, the all-weather paved path leads to a living maze of over 800 arborvitae trees. The evergreen maze was visually designed to wave in the wind and gates were placed so that the paths could be altered for added interest for repeat visitors.

A continual work in progress, new gardens are planned and will be added over time. Charley Creek Gardens is a delightful place for unhurried visits in all seasons.

*Charley Creek Gardens, 551 N. Miami St., Wabash, IN 46992 **Tel:** (260) 563-1020 **Web:** www.charleycreekgardens.org **Open:** grounds daily, dawn to dusk **Acreage:** 10 **Fee(s):** guided tours, facility rental **Botanical Collections:** native wildflowers, grasses, bog plants, herbs, greenhouse, labyrinths, annuals, perennials, water features, sculpture, garden ornaments.

Waterfall, Charley Creek Gardens, Wabash

Purdue University Horticulture Gardens

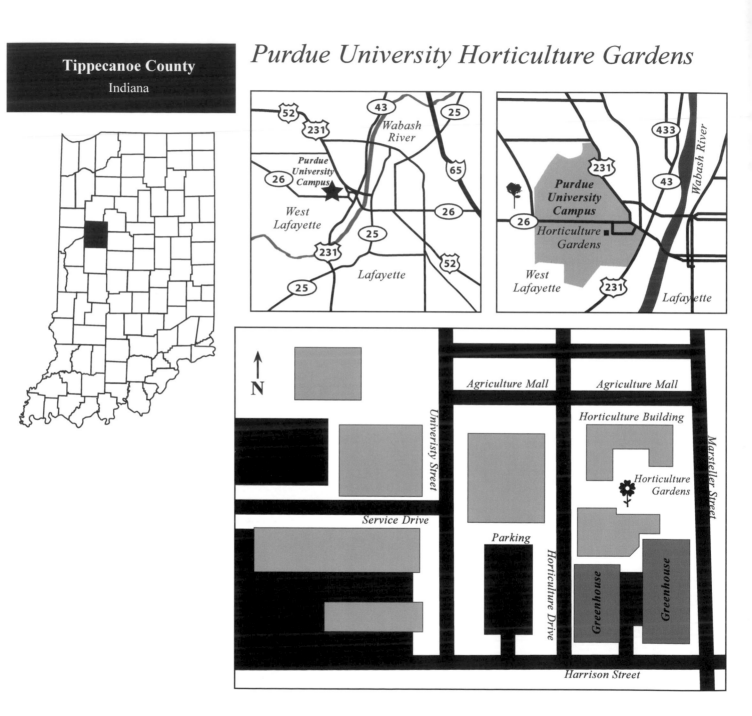

Tippecanoe County
Indiana

Wabash River

Purdue University Campus

West Lafayette

Lafayette

Purdue University Campus

Horticulture Gardens

West Lafayette

Lafayette

Wabash River

N

Agriculture Mall

Agriculture Mall

University Street

Horticulture Building

Horticulture Gardens

Service Drive

Parking

Horticulture Drive

Greenhouse

Greenhouse

Marsteller Street

Harrison Street

19. PURDUE UNIVERSITY HORTICULTURE GARDENS
WEST LAFAYETTE, INDIANA

> *"No occupation is so delightful to me as the culture of the earth, and no culture comparable to that of a garden."*
>
> **Thomas Jefferson**

Established in 1982, the half acre Horticulture Gardens at Purdue University features an array of award-winning annuals, perennials, and vegetable garden cultivars where a walk through is a pleasure and an education. Maintained by students and volunteers, over 200 species of perennials and 300 cultivars are displayed and labeled in this "living classroom." Special collections include peonies, daylilies, hostas, spring flowering bulbs and ornamental grasses. Recently a new cedar wood pavilion was constructed in the midst of the lovely setting and several of the beds were redesigned by landscape architectural students and planted with floral splendor.

A self-guided tour brochure is available at the garden's entrance. Group tours may be arranged by appointment. The Horticulture Department and Master Gardeners host the annual Purdue Garden Day Open House each summer with garden tours and educational programs. Friends of the Gardens help financially with donations to the Purdue Foundation. The Horticulture Gardens are situated on the campus of Purdue University at the Horticulture Building's east entrance at the corner of Wood and Marstellar streets at 625 Agricultural Mall.

While visiting Purdue's campus, consider walking the three color-coded tree tours that identify 100 of the trees growing on campus. A pamphlet entitled Trees of Purdue University is available. In addition, Horticulture Park, located at the west end of campus features several labeled trees and pathways.

*Purdue University Horticulture Gardens, 625 Agriculture Mall Dr. & Marstellar St., West Lafayette, IN 47907-1165 **Tel:** (765) 494-1300 Hort. Bldg., 494-1296 tours **Web:** www.hort.purdue.edu **Open:** daily, daylight hours **Acreage:** 0.5 gardens **Fee(s):** donations accepted, garden membership **Botanical Collections:** ornamental display garden, annuals, perennials, vegetable garden display.

Colorful Annuals,
Purdue University Horticulture Gardens, West Lafayette

Christy Woods

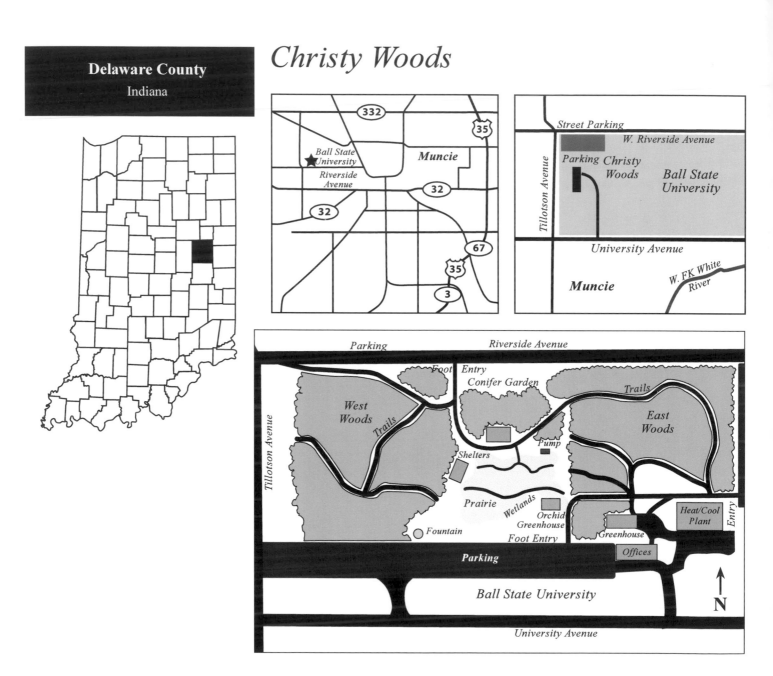

Delaware County
Indiana

332

35

Ball State
University

Muncie

Riverside
Avenue

32

32

67

35

3

Street Parking

W. Riverside Avenue

Parking Christy
Woods

Ball State
University

Tillotson Avenue

University Avenue

Muncie

W. FK White
River

Parking

Riverside Avenue

Foot Entry
Conifer Garden

Trails

West
Woods
Trails

East
Woods

Pump

Tillotson Avenue

Shelters

Prairie

Wetlands

Orchid
Greenhouse
Foot Entry

Heat/Cool
Plant

Entry

Greenhouse

Fountain

Offices

Parking

Ball State University

N

University Avenue

20. CHRISTY WOODS
MUNCIE, INDIANA

> *"I think I shall never see, a poem lovely as a tree."*
>
> *Joyce Kilmer*

Since 1919, Christy Woods has been a teaching "laboratory" for Ball State University, Muncie and surrounding communities. Under the direction of the biology department, science professor, Dr. O. B. Christy promoted the idea of preserving the former farm pastured woodlot for educational purposes. Recognizing the property's educational potential, the Ball brothers purchased and donated the property to the university. Native trees, shrubs and wildflowers were transplanted to the site for restoration. Since 2000, the 17 acre preserve has been designated a Field Station and Environmental Center.

Nearly two-thirds of Christy Woods is eastern deciduous forest, divided at the middle of the property into East Woods and West Woods. A network of interconnecting, short, self-guiding trails with wildflower and tree names weave through the woodland. Located at the center of the preserve is the Conifer Garden, tall grass Prairie Area (30 species) wetlands, the Wheeler Orchid Collection Greenhouse (1,200 specimens) and the 3,400 square foot Teaching and Research Greenhouse (3,000 tropical, desert, aquatic specimens). Both greenhouses are open for viewing when staff is on duty. Free guided tours are available. Brochures and booklets about the greenhouse are available as well as *A Field Guide to the Spring Wildflowers of Christy Woods* and *A Field Guide to the Woody Plants of Christy Woods.*

Christy Woods is located at the southwest edge of campus just west of the Cooper Science Building. Christy Woods is bordered north by Riverside Avenue (free street side parking), west by Tillotson Avenue, and south by the University Avenue parking lot. Visitors are required to obtain a free temporary parking tag to park in designated university parking lots Monday through Friday, but weekend parking is permit free in the south University Avenue parking lot where restrooms and sheltered picnicking are available. There are three foot-access entry gates: Riverside Avenue North Gate, Nature Study East Gate, and the South Pedestrian Gate.

Beech Path, East Wood,
Christy Woods, Ball State University, Muncie

*Christy Woods (between Riverside, Tillotson & University avenues) Dept. of Biology, Ball State University, Muncie, IN 47306 **Tel:** (765) 285-8820, (765) 285-2641 **Web:** www.bsu.edu/fseec/environment **Open:** Mon.-Fri. 7:30 a.m.-4:30 p.m., Sat. 10 a.m.-3 p.m., Sun. 1:00-5:00 p.m. (April 1-Oct. 31) **Acreage:** 17 **Fee(s):** donations accepted **Botanical Collections:** orchids, tropical, desert, aquatic greenhouses, arboretum, conifers, prairie, wildflowers, wetlands.

Oakhurst Gardens & Minnetrista Cultural Center

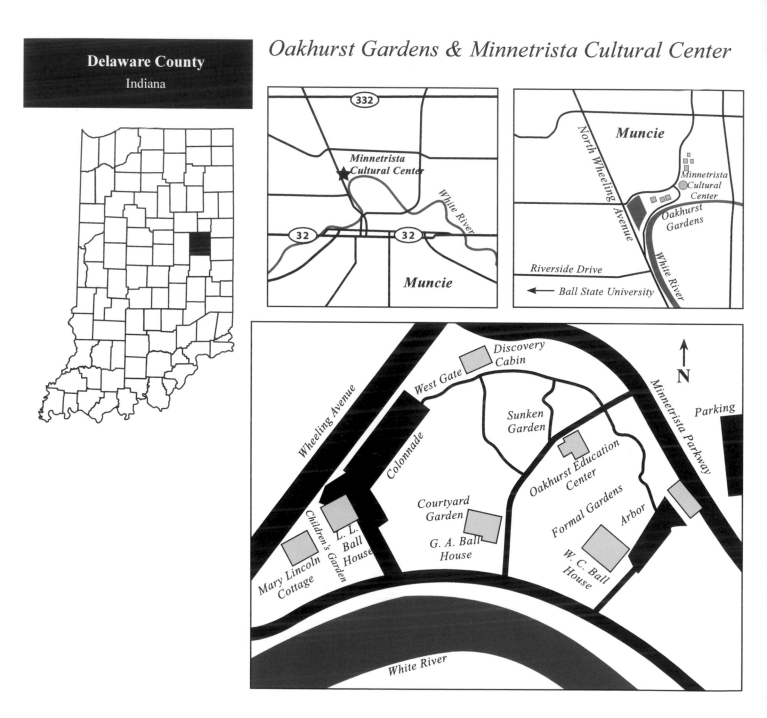

Delaware County
Indiana

332

Minnetrista
Cultural Center

White River

32   32

Muncie

North Wheeling Avenue

Muncie

Minnetrista
Cultural
Center

Oakhurst
Gardens

White River

Riverside Drive

← Ball State University

Wheeling Avenue

West Gate

Discovery
Cabin

Sunken
Garden

Colonnade

Oakhurst Education
Center

Minnetrista Parkway

Parking

N

Children's Garden

L. L.
Ball
House

Courtyard
Garden

Formal Gardens

Arbor

Mary Lincoln
Cottage

G. A. Ball
House

W. C. Ball
House

White River

21. OAKHURST GARDENS
MUNCIE, INDIANA

Located north of downtown Muncie along the White River West Fork, Oakhurst was the former family home of George and Frances Ball and their daughter, Elisabeth, who majored in botany at Vassar College. From 1895 to 1970, the formal and natural gardens were developed by Frances and Elisabeth. After falling into disuse in the latter 20th century, the historic house and gardens were restored to their former splendor by the Minnetrista Cultural Center and opened to the public in 1995.

Children's Garden, Oakhurst Gardens, Muncie

The 6.5 acres of formal gardens surrounding the Oakhurst home include Aunt Emma's Path, an array of perennial and annual flower beds, a wooden arbor, a number of garden sculptures of historic significance to the property, Formal Garden, the Courtyard Garden, the Doll House (a replica of Elisabeth's childhood playhouse), a multi-themed Children's Garden, Sunken Garden and Colonnade Garden.

In addition, a Rose Garden featuring a wrought iron gazebo purchased at the 1939 New York World's Fair is located adjacent south of the Minnetrista Cultural Center. A variety of hybrid tea roses and English roses surround the gazebo. Also of further interest is the eight acre Nature Area, planted with Indiana natives that include habitats such as a tall grass prairie, upland deciduous forest and a freshwater pond, located north of the Minnestrista Cultural Center and Saint Joseph Street, next to the Minnetrista Parkway.

Additional facilities and events include the Minnestrista Cultural Center Shop/museum store, Orchard Shop, the seasonal Farmer's Market and a rich variety of cultural events and educational programs throughout the year. All tours begin at Minnetrista.

*Oakhurst Gardens at Minnetrista (located between Wheeling Ave. and North Walnut St.), 1200 N. Minnetrista Parkway, Muncie, IN 47303 **Tel:** (765) 282-4848 or (800) 428-5887 **Web:** www.minnetrista.net **Open:** Mon.-Sat., 9 a.m.-5:30 p.m., Sun. 11 a.m.-5:30 p.m., closed New Year's Day, Easter, Thanksgiving Day & Christmas day

Acreage: 6 gardens, 40 grounds **Fee(s):** none for gardens, admission to cultural center, special events **Botanical Collections:** restored historic estate formal gardens, rose garden, children's gardens, native plants, bird & butterfly garden, culinary herb garden, woodland garden, annual display gardens.

> *"Nothing is more completely the child of art than a garden."*
> **Sir Walter Scott**

Arts Park Garden

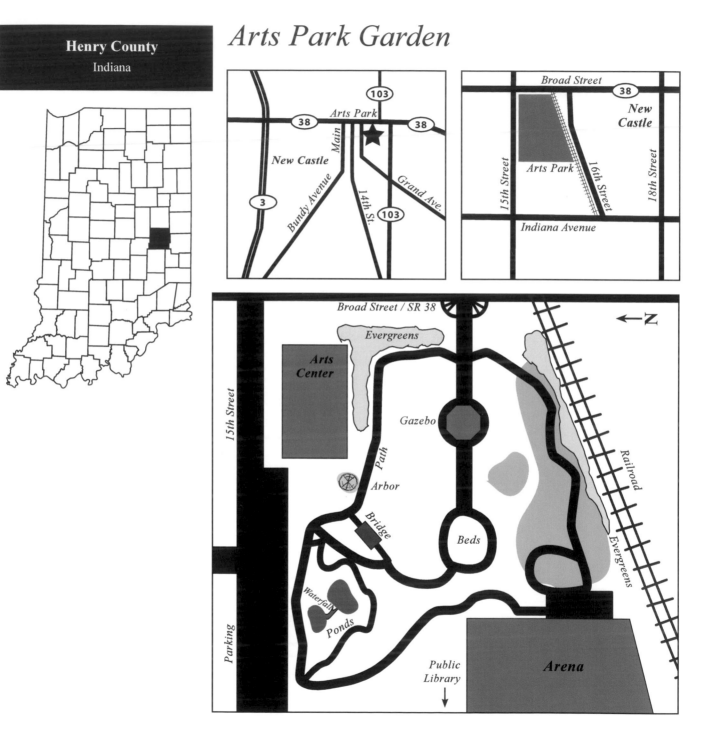

Henry County
Indiana

103

38

Arts Park

38

New Castle

Main

Bundy Avenue

3

14th St.

Grand Ave.

103

Broad Street

38

New Castle

15th Street

Arts Park

16th Street

18th Street

Indiana Avenue

Broad Street / SR 38

N

Evergreens

Arts Center

15th Street

Gazebo

Path

Arbor

Bridge

Beds

Railroad

Evergreens

Waterfall

Ponds

Parking

Public Library

Arena

> *"Gardening is the slowest of the performing arts."*
> **Anonymous**

Arts Park Garden began in 1995 when the ambitious members of the Arts Association of Henry County decided to develop the remainder of their donated and purchased, three acre, inner city property into a park to complement their newly dedicated Art Center. From 1995 to 1999, the park site was prepared for landscaping with extensive demolition and excavation of several derelict buildings that occupied the future green space. In the spirit of community cooperation, a design was adopted with the goal of providing a downtown public garden park just a short walking distance from the county courthouse and city library.

By 2002 Arts Park Garden was completed, but continues, as most gardens, a work in progress. The contribution of thousands of hours by dedicated volunteer gardeners have made Arts Park a rewarding place for all to visit and a role model for every Indiana community to emulate.

Elements of the garden park include beds of flowering annuals and perennials that form drifts of blazing color amidst the carpet of green lawn; over 150 flowering, shade, and evergreen trees that provide picturesque seasonal color, decoration and welcome relief from the summer sun; twin ponds filled with water lilies, hyacinth, iris, lotus and goldfish are connected by a cascading waterfall that add to the cool green retreat.

Arts Park Overlook, New Castle

The gazebo and vine-covered iron arbors beckon visitors and dazzle the eye. Oriental influences are noted in the arch bridge over a dry steam filled with boulders. A wall of evergreen trees and other plant materials screen the railroad on the south border of the park. Shrubs and ornamental grasses line the stone walkways and cover the mounded areas. The 1890 antique iron gates at the Broad Street/S.R. 38 entrance welcome the public. The 22,000 square foot Arena is located at the South Gate entry and parking area and is the scene of special cultural public events as well as private celebrations such as wedding receptions. The North Gate entry at the 15th Street parking lot is the high point of the garden park and provides a sweeping view of the fanciful place. There are several benches and picnic table that have thoughtfully been placed amidst the visually stunning gardens.

From eyesore to beauty spot, the magical union of art and garden has had an uplifting effect on the neighborhood and the community. Arts Park is a garden centerpiece that offers visitors a delight-filled place to rest and refresh.

*Arts Park Garden, (located between Broad Street/S.R. 38, 15th & 16th Sts.), 218 S. 15th St., New Castle, IN 47362 **Tel:** (765) 529-2634 **Web:** www.aachci.org **Open:** daily, daylight hours **Acreage:** nearly 3 **Fee(s):** facility rental, special events & programs **Botanical Collections:** formal flower gardens, annuals, perennials, trees, shrubs, grasses, aquatic plants.

Richmond Rose Gardens

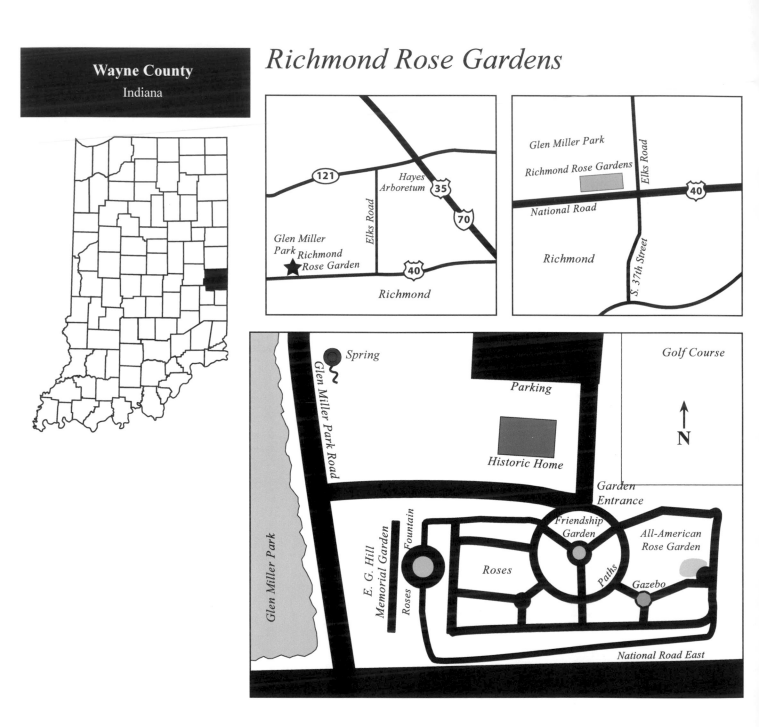

Wayne County

Indiana

121

Hayes Arboretum

35

70

Elks Road

Glen Miller Park

Richmond Rose Garden

40

Richmond

Glen Miller Park

Richmond Rose Gardens

Elks Road

40

National Road

S. 37th Street

Richmond

Spring

Glen Miller Park Road

Glen Miller Park

Parking

Historic Home

Golf Course

N

Garden Entrance

E. G. Hill Memorial Garden

Fountain

Roses

Roses

Friendship Garden

Paths

All-American Rose Garden

Gazebo

National Road East

23. RICHMOND ROSE GARDENS
RICHMOND, INDIANA

*Victorian Gazebo Centerpiece,
Richmond Rose Gardens, Richmond*

Adopting the slogan, "The Rose City," Richmond has historically been a center of the cut rose industry. Located in 194 acre Glen Miller Park are three adjoining, but separate public rose gardens that honor the community's commercial rose heritage. Early June to September is the peak bloom time to visit the gracious setting.

Dedicated in 1937, the E. G. Hill Memorial Rose Garden honors rosarian Guerney Hill, an early Richmond rose hybridizer and co-founder of Hill Floral Products, one of the nation's largest producers of cut roses. *Madame Butterfly, Columbia, Richmond* and *Premier* are some of the best known rose hybrids created by Mr. Hill. Over 200 roses are planted in the Victorian-styled garden which includes a pergola and fountain center. The garden is maintained by the Richmond Parks and Recreation Department and forms the outer west border of the three rose gardens.

Occupying the east border of the rose gardens is the All-American Rose Display Garden. Established in 1987, this rose garden is one of two in Indiana to have earned the All-American Rose Display Garden distinction (Lakeside Rose Garden, Fort Wayne is the second), and one of 139 A. A. R. S. public display rose gardens in the nation. The European and Victorian designed garden has room for up to 2,000 roses and represents 110 varieties. Flowering annuals, perennials, evergreen, flowering and shade trees are also included in the kaleidoscope of color. Historic brick pathways access the gardens that are centered about a Victorian gazebo. The All-American Rose Display Garden is a community-wide project and volunteers maintain the gardens that are funded by public contributions.

In the center of the floral display, the Richmond-Friendship Garden honors the rose relationship with Zweibruken, Germany. Established in 1992, the garden is designed by James Brower of Gaar Nurseries and displays over 120 roses, many German in origin from the Europas Rosegarten of Zweibruken. The centerpiece is a sculpture that symbolizes their friendship between the two cities. The Friendship Garden is maintained by an all volunteer group and is a community-wide project.

The Richmond Rose Gardens are located at 2500 National Road East/U. S. 40 near the south entrance of Glen Miller Park. The rose gardens are at the east side of the lower park drive adjacent to the golf course. Parking is available north of the historic Charles House, which may be rented, along with the Victorian gazebo for weddings and special events. Glen Miller Park, Richmond's premier park, offers picnicking and other amenities including several floral display beds scattered throughout the park's landscape.

> "Every rose is an autograph from the hand of God on his world about us."
> **Theodore Parker**

*Richmond Rose Gardens, Glen Miller Park, 2500 National Rd./ U.S. 40 East, Richmond, IN 47374 **Tel:** (765) 962-1638, 983-7275 **Web:** www.waynet.org **Open:** daily, 7 a.m.-11 p.m. **Acreage:** 1 **Fee(s):** donations accepted, facility rental, guided tours **Botanical Collections:** formal rose gardens, All-American Rose Selection Display Garden, annuals, perennials, ornamental & shade trees.

Hayes Arboretum

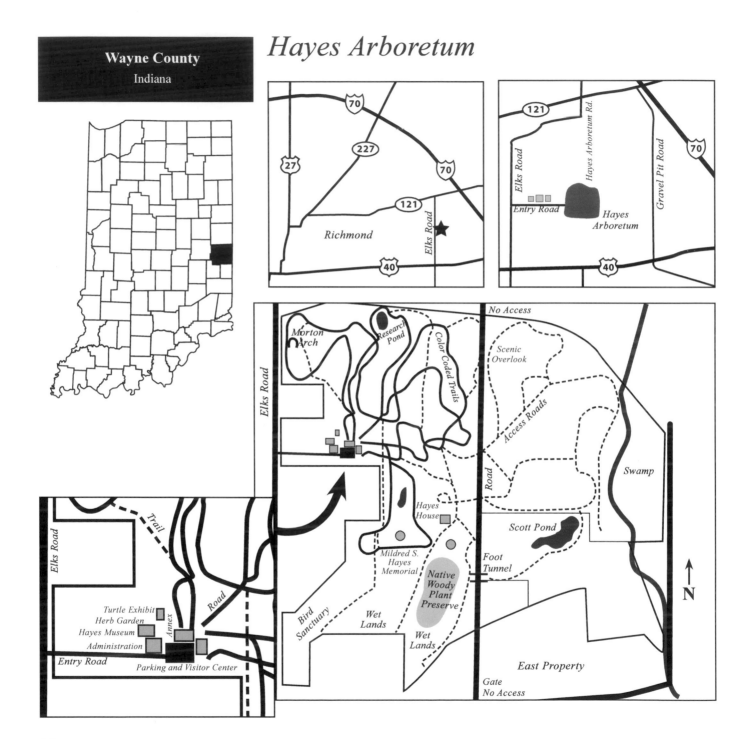

Wayne County
Indiana

70
227
27
121
70
Richmond
Elks Road
40

121
70
Elks Road
Hayes Arboretum Rd.
Gravel Pit Road
Entry Road
Hayes Arboretum
40

No Access
Morton Arch
Research Pond
Color Coded Trails
Scenic Overlook
Access Roads
Swamp
Road
Elks Road
Hayes House
Scott Pond
Mildred S. Hayes Memorial
Foot Tunnel
Native Woody Plant Preserve
Bird Sanctuary
Wet Lands
Wet Lands
East Property
Gate No Access
N

Trail
Elks Road
Road
Turtle Exhibit
Herb Garden
Hayes Museum
Annex
Administration
Entry Road
Parking and Visitor Center

24. HAYES ARBORETUM
RICHMOND, INDIANA

> *"Heaven and earth help him who plants a tree, and his work its own reward shall be."*
> **Lucy Larcom**

Hayes Arboretum is the educational outreach project of the Stanley Wolcott Hayes Research Foundation, a private, non-profit organization, whose mission is "to provide nature and recreational related education." Beginning in 1930, Stanley W. Hayes (1865-1963), railroad official and inventor, purchased an old homestead farm in northeast Richmond and began native reforestation of the vacant fields, created experimental forestry plots and protected the existing natural heritage. Since the Hayes Arboretum opened in 1963, the 466 acre preserve has actively engaged in environmental education, outdoor recreation and scientific research in order to promote awareness and appreciation of Indiana's natural resources.

Visitors begin their visit to Hayes Arboretum at the nature center, a renovated 1833 dairy barn that offers information, interpretive displays, restrooms and drinking water. West, across the parking lot from the nature center, are the Hayes Museum and administrative offices, an herb garden, a butterfly house, a turtle pen and other displays.

Four color-coded loop trails that total three miles begin behind the nature center, accessing the secluded areas of the beech-maple forest on the 177 acre west side of the arboretum. The Auto Tour also begins at the nature center where a drive through is a delight and an education. Sixty acres of virgin old-growth forest with trees up to 450 years old are located along the Red and Blue trails.

The one mile History Trail leads visitors to the scenic Brice E. Hayes Memorial Fountain and the ten-acre Paul C. McClure Native Woody Plant Preserve where one or more specimens of every indigenous woody plant (179 species) of the Whitewater Valley and its tributaries are exhibited. Just east of the woody plant preserve is a tunnel under Hayes Arboretum Road that provides foot access to the 175 acre east side of the arboretum. Additional features of Hayes Arboretum include a Woodland Chapel, Springhouse Shelter, the Hayes House, Mildred S. Hayes Memorial, Adena and Hopewell Indian mounds, ponds, fields, wetlands and educational programs and classes.

Hayes Arboretum is reached from I-70 by exiting 156A and driving west two miles on the National Road/U. S. 40 to Elks Road. Turn north on Elks Road and proceed 0.5 miles to the arboretum's main entrance and the nature center.

*Hayes Arboretum, 801 Elks Rd., Richmond, IN 47374 **Tel:** (765) 962-3745 **Web:** www.hayesarboretum.org **Open:** March 1- November 1, Tues.-Sat. 9:00 a.m.-5:00, open only for special events & programs November through February **Acreage:** 466 **Fee(s):** auto tour, facility rental, group tours, educational programs, special events, membership available **Botanical Collections:** arboretum, native plants, herb garden, butterfly garden.

Brice Hayes Memorial Fountain, Hayes Arboretum, Richmond

Coxhall Gardens

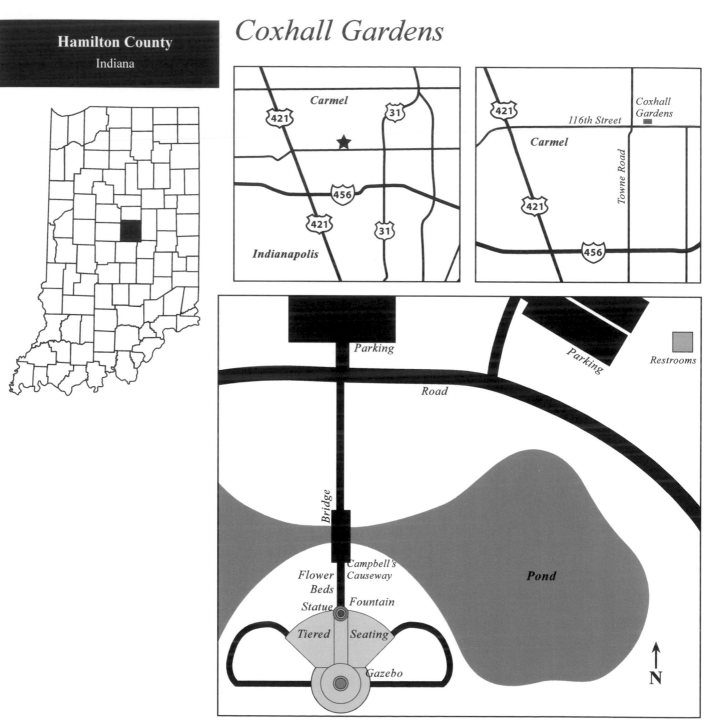

Hamilton County
Indiana

Carmel

421

31

456

421

31

Indianapolis

421

116th Street

Coxhall Gardens

Carmel

Towne Road

421

456

Parking

Parking

Restrooms

Road

Bridge

Campbell's
Causeway

Flower
Beds

Statue

Fountain

Tiered

Seating

Pond

Gazebo

N

25. COXHALL GARDENS
CARMEL, INDIANA

Coxhall Gardens, a Hamilton County Park, had its origins in donated land and three homes from Jesse H. and Beulah Cox in 1999. The 125 acre suburban garden park is a work in progress, scheduled to be completed in 2010 at a cost of $30 million dollars. Future plans include numerous ornate specialty theme gardens

"[Coxhall]An oasis in a sea of homes."
Jesse H. Cox

such as an English Garden, Italian Renaissance Garden and a European Formal Garden as well as a museum and conservatory. Currently, the picturesque landscape with its sweeping lawn vistas has begun its transformation into one of Indiana's most beautiful public gardens.

Two 90-foot-high bell tower carillons welcome visitors at the Towne Road west entrance and the Hoover Road east entrance. The centerpiece of the gardens is an elegant gazebo, fountain, waterfall, tiered lawn seating for special gathering, and a statue of the garden donors. Connected to the impressive centerpiece is the Campbell Crossing or causeway, a gracious landscaped bridge setting overlooking a lake. The nearby Children's Garden includes "Village Stores," "Tiki Huts," "Echo Wells", "Grasshopper Maze", and "Peek-a-Boo Hills." Winding paths weave throughout the open green space and restrooms are available.

To reach Coxhall Gardens from I-465, exit 31 onto U. S. 31 and drive north 1.75 miles to 116th Street and turn west. Follow 116th Street west about 2.25 miles to Towne Road or about two miles to Hoover Road and turn north. Continue on Towne Road about 0.5 mile to the west garden entrance and on Hoover Road less than 0.5 mile to the east garden entrance.

Campbell's Crossing, Coxhall Gardens, Carmel

*Coxhall Gardens, 2000 W. 116th St. & Towne Rd., Carmel, IN 46032 **Tel:** (317) 896-5874 **Web:** www.co.hamilton.in.us/parks or coxhall@co.hamilton.in.us **Open:** daily, daylight hours **Acreage:** 125 **Fee(s):** donations accepted, facility rental, special events **Botanical Collections:** annuals, perennials, flowering trees, shade trees.

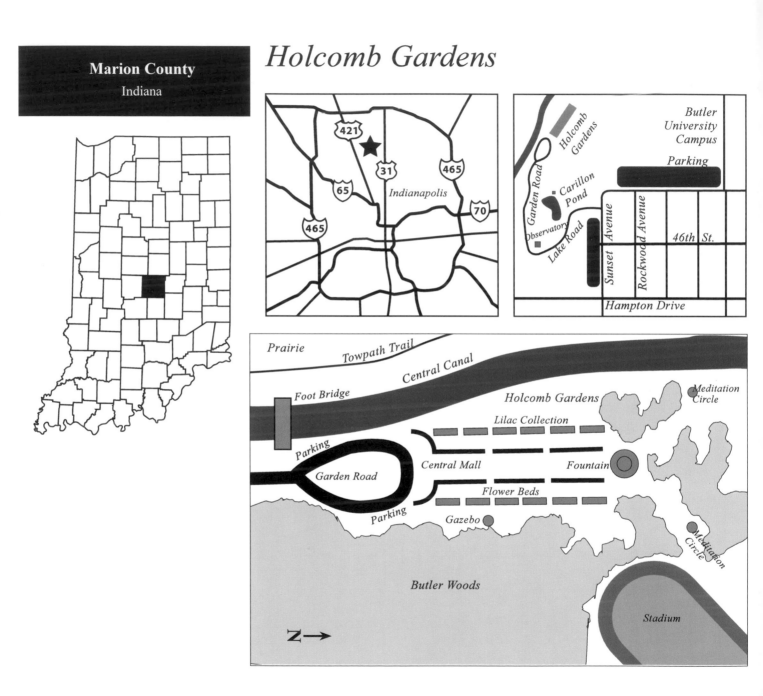

Holcomb Gardens

Marion County
Indiana

421
31
465
65
Indianapolis
465
70

Holcomb Gardens
Garden Road
Carillon Pond
Observatory
Lake Road
Sunset Avenue
Rockwood Avenue
46th St.
Butler University Campus
Parking
Hampton Drive

Prairie
Towpath Trail
Central Canal
Foot Bridge
Holcomb Gardens
Meditation Circle
Lilac Collection
Parking
Garden Road
Central Mall
Fountain
Flower Beds
Parking
Gazebo
Meditation Circle
Butler Woods
Stadium
N→

26. HOLCOMB GARDENS
INDIANAPOLIS, INDIANA

Holcomb Gardens, situated at the north edge of the Butler University campus, began in 1920 and is named in honor of James Irving Holcomb, a former university vice-president and Indianapolis industrialist. The 20-acre gardens are positioned on a level grassy plain between the Indianapolis Water Company Central Canal and Butler Woods.

> *"The garden must be prepared in the soul first or else it will not flourish."*
>
> **English Proverb**

Looking north from the shaded parking area, the Central Garden Mall presents a dramatic sweeping lawn, flanked by long rectangular beds of flowering annuals and perennials, bordered further by a variety of flowering trees and shrubs such as crabapples and lilacs. After several years of decline, the lilac collection is being restored. During the warmer months, the mall is the scene of weddings and bridal portraits.

A focal point at the north end of Central Mall is an elegant water fountain with a statue of Persephone, a Greek goddess of mythology who represents the personification of spring. Just beyond the fountain beneath shaded tree groves are sitting areas where reflective inscriptions from the Great Teachers such as Plato, Shakespeare and Jesus are carved into stone and statuary figureheads overlooking the spacious grounds. A carillon, waterfall and reflecting pond are situated at a wooded knoll at the edge of the ten-acre Butler Woods, southeast of the gardens and northeast of the of the Holcomb Observatory and Planetarium.

Across the Central Canal west via foot bridges is the three acre Butler Prairie which has served as an outdoor educational resource since 1987. The prairie is located south of the playing fields and next to the radio tower. Best time to visit is late summer and early fall.

In addition, the Butler Tree Campus Walk begins at the Holcomb Gardens gate where a large American Beech is identified as number one of thirty trees. A brochure and map are available. Also, of further botanic interest is the small medicinal herb garden that has been established alongside the sidewalk north of the Pharmacy Building.

*Holcomb Gardens, Butler University, 4600 Sunset Ave., Indianapolis, IN 46208 **Tel:** (317) 283-9413, 283-8000 **Web:** info@butler.edu **Open:** daily, daylight hours **Acreage:** 20 **Fee(s):** none **Botanical Collections:** formal display gardens, fountain, statuary, carillon, medicinal herb garden, prairie.

Central Mall, Holcomb Gardens, Butler University, Indianapolis

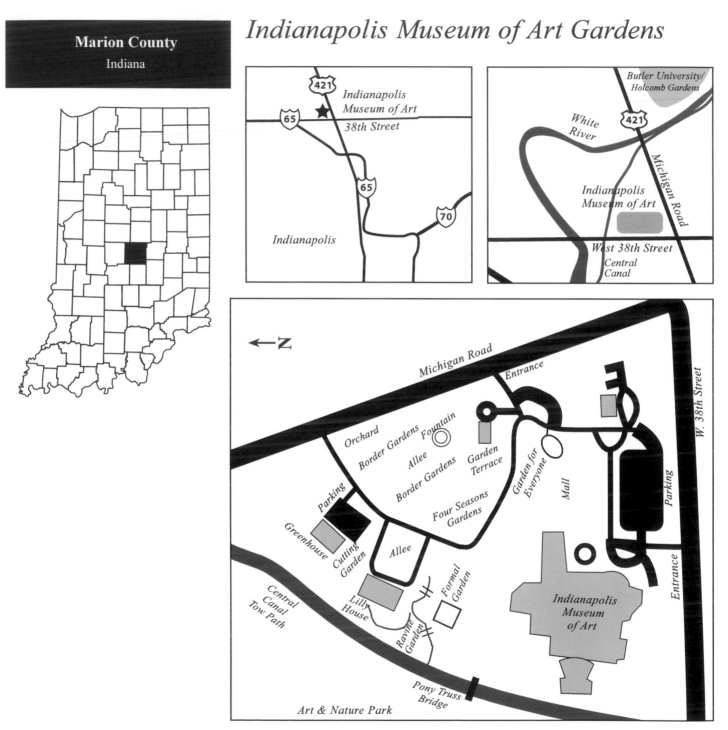

Indianapolis Museum of Art Gardens

Marion County
Indiana

421
65
Indianapolis
Museum of Art
38th Street
65
70
Indianapolis

Butler University/
Holcomb Gardens
White
River
421
Michigan Road
Indianapolis
Museum of Art
West 38th Street
Central
Canal

←N

Michigan Road
Entrance
Orchard
Border Gardens
Fountain
Allee
Border Gardens
Garden
Terrace
Garden for Everyone
Mall
W. 38th Street
Parking
Four Seasons
Gardens
Greenhouse
Cutting
Garden
Allee
Parking
Lilly
House
Formal
Garden
Entrance
Central
Canal
Tow Path
Ravine
Garden
Indianapolis
Museum
of Art
Pony Truss
Bridge
Art & Nature Park

27. INDIANAPOLIS MUSEUM OF ART GARDENS

INDIANAPOLIS, INDIANA

> *"Gardens are the result of a collaboration between art and nature."*
> **Penelope Hobhouse**

The grounds surrounding the Indianapolis Museum of Art showcases a group of modern and historic gardens in which art and nature merge harmoniously. For the horticultural visitor, numerous walkways and foot paths lead to some of Indiana's most interesting garden gems, including areas surrounding the museum, the Garden for Everyone, Oldfields-Lilly Mansion and Gardens, the Madeline F. Elder Greenhouse and Garden Shop, and the Virginia B. Fairbanks Art and Nature Park.

The Plaza Garden features a rich variety of labeled shade and flowering trees with colorful beds of annuals and perennials beneath, enclosing the parking area and provide a stunning welcome entry to the art museum. Fountains and sculpture, including the ever-popular Robert Indiana's LOVE sculpture, grace the elegant setting.

Just southeast of the tree-lined Sutphin Mall is the Garden for Everyone. As its name implies, the garden was designed to be accessible and enjoyable for all. With its soothing fountain and raised beds displaying plants in a wide variety of colors, textures and fragrances, the Garden for Everyone provides delights for all the senses.

Following North Drive past the Garden Terrace and the Four Seasons Garden, visitors will arrive at Oldfields-Lilly House and Garden, a 26-acre American Country Place era estate and National Historic Landmark. Built by Indianapolis businessman Hugh Landon in 1910 and purchased by J. K. Lilly, Jr. in 1932, Oldfields features a French chateau-style mansion and gardens designed by landscape architect Percival Gallagher, an associate of Olmsted Brothers of Brookline, Massachusetts, in the 1920s.

Gallagher's contributions include a grand allee of red oaks extending from the mansion to a circular fountain pool, a sculptural group of *The Three Graces*, meandering border gardens and a one-acre ravine garden with a cascading stream, rock pools and beautiful plantings. Another highlight is the formal garden that features white–painted arbors, geometrically arranged flowerbeds and a central fountain.

North and east of the Lilly house is the Madeline F. Elder Greenhouse that offers seasonal plant displays, an extensive orchid collection, and a retail garden shop that is open year around.

West from Oldfields-Lilly Mansion and Gardens, across the Central Canal is the 100-acre Virginia B. Fairbanks Art and Nature Park. A pony truss bridge over the canal provides access to a wooded area and 30-acre man-made lake. The art and nature park opens fall 2009 and will feature contemporary art in a naturalistic setting. Additional gardens and facilities include a rock garden, dwarf conifer collection, orchard, gift shops, library and restaurants. A map of the gardens is available.

*Indianapolis Museum of Art Gardens**, 4000 Michigan Rd. & 1200 W. 38th St., Indianapolis, IN 46208 **Tel:** (317) 923-1331, group tours 920-2679 **Web:** www.ima-art.org **Open:** gardens open daily, dawn to dusk **Acreage:** 26 gardens, 152 grounds **Fee(s):** workshops, classes, programs, special events, garden/museum membership **Botanical Collections:** estate garden, thematic gardens, allee, fountains, statuary.

Formal Garden, Oldfields Estate, Indianapolis Museum of Art

White River Gardens

Marion County
Indiana

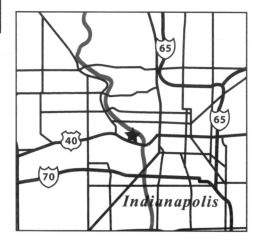

Indianapolis

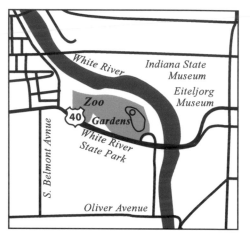

White River

Indiana State Museum

Eiteljorg Museum

Zoo Gardens

S. Belmont Avnue

White River State Park

Oliver Avenue

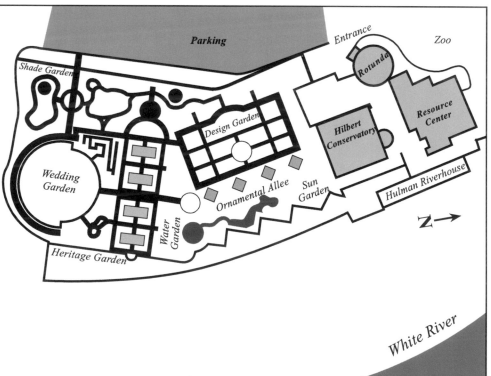

Parking

Entrance

Zoo

Shade Garden

Rotunda

Design Garden

Hilbert Conservatory

Resource Center

Wedding Garden

Ornamental Allee

Sun Garden

Hulman Riverhouse

Water Garden

Z→

Heritage Garden

White River

28. WHITE RIVER GARDENS
INDIANAPOLIS, INDIANA

> *"Flowers are just moments of gratification."*
>
> *Kevin Doyle*

Located just west of downtown Indianapolis in White River State Park, the White River Gardens were established in 1999 and were created in the interest of furthering education and personal application and enjoyment of gardening. In proportion to its size of 3.3 acres, these urban gardens are rich in delightful horticultural displays that are designed to provide pleasure and learning experiences.

From the parking area, visitors enter through the silo-styled Schaefer Rotunda where a 360-degree mural, "Midwestern Panorama" encircles the wall. Within the enclosed complex is the Gardeners Pride gift shop, Flora Café, the Hulman Riverhouse meeting room and the Dick Crum Resource Center where professional horticulturalists find answers to gardener's questions.

After paying admission, visitors enter the 5,000-square-foot, 65-foot-high, glass-enclosed Hilbert Conservatory. The barn-shaped conservatory contains numerous tropical and subtropical plant species and features special seasonal exhibitions.

Beyond the conservatory doors is the DeHaan Tiergarten, a collection of 18 theme gardens that combine beauty with botany, all accessible along 1.5 miles of pathways. Within this dramatic creation are 11 design gardens, a Shade Garden, a Water Garden, a Wedding Garden, a Sun-Stream-Prairie Garden plus an ornamental tree-lined allee and belvedere vista point. In addition, there is a Knot Garden, a Heritage Garden and a Hedge Garden. Over 1,000 varieties of plants are easily identified by labels or by available gardeners. The adjacent zoo also displays plants in ecological settings.

Knot Garden, White River Gardens, Indianapolis

*White River Gardens, 1200 W. Washington St./U.S. 40 (next to the Indianapolis Zoo), P. O. Box 22309, Indianapolis, IN 46222-0309   **Tel:** (317) 630-2001, 2045, 1-800-665-9056   **Web:** www.whiterivergardens.com   **Open:** seasonal hours vary; Jan.-Feb., 9 a.m.- 4 p.m.; Wed.-Sun, closed Mon. & Tues.; Mar.-Nov., daily, 9 a.m.- 4 p.m. longer closing time on weekends; Dec., noon- 9 p.m. daily; closed Thanksgiving Day, Christmas Even & Day, New Year's Eve & Day   **Acreage:** 3.3   **Fee(s):** admission (includes zoo), parking, facility rental, lectures, classes, programs, workshops, special events, garden membership   **Botanical Collections:** conservatory, demonstration gardens, theme gardens.

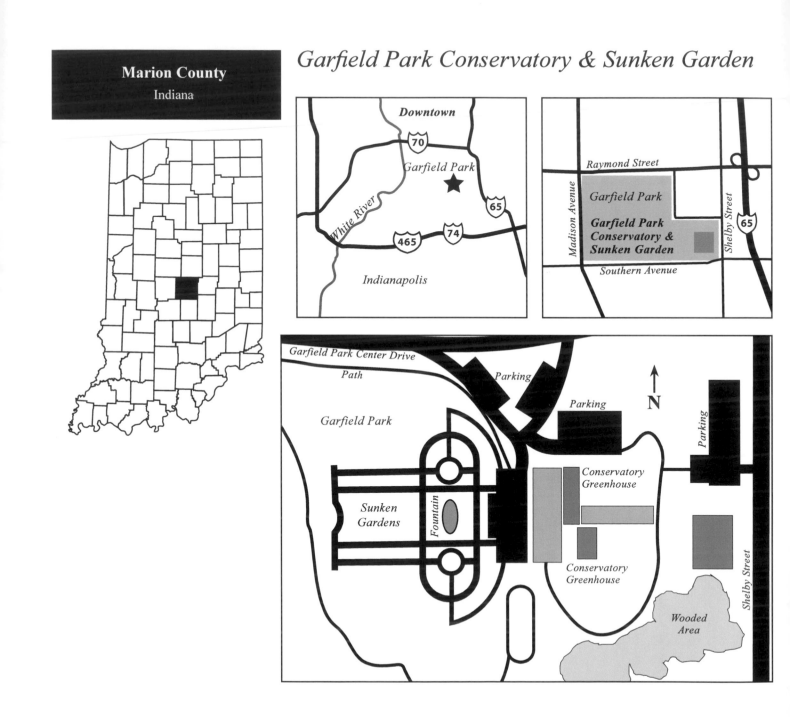

Garfield Park Conservatory & Sunken Garden

Marion County
Indiana

Downtown

70

Garfield Park

65

White River

465   74

Indianapolis

Raymond Street

Madison Avenue

Garfield Park

Garfield Park Conservatory & Sunken Garden

Shelby Street

65

Southern Avenue

Garfield Park Center Drive

Path

Parking

Garfield Park

Parking

N

Parking

Sunken Gardens

Fountain

Conservatory Greenhouse

Conservatory Greenhouse

Wooded Area

Shelby Street

29. GARFIELD PARK CONSERVATORY & SUNKEN GARDEN
INDIANAPOLIS, INDIANA

Established in 1873, Garfield Park, named in honor of President James A. Garfield, was the first Indianapolis city park. The Conservatory and Sunken Garden are one of Indiana's oldest and historically-significant botanic garden parks.

In 1914, under the director of George E. Kessler, landscape architect and superintendent of the Indianapolis Department of Parks, the planning of the Sunken Garden and Conservatory began. Kessler's academic background in botany, landscape design and civil engineering gave him skills to design a botanic site similar to the Royal Gardens of Europe. Kessler was an important figure in the "City Beautiful" movement.

In 1915, the overlook of the Sunken Garden was completed and in 1916, the fountains were installed, and at that time, it was the largest lighted fountain display in the United States. Formal Victorian plantings and brick walks were placed around the fountains. The sunken garden was dedicated and opened to the public on October 29, 1916.

> *"Every flower is a soul blossoming out of nature."*
> **Gerald de Narval**

The original Victorian-styled conservatory was erected and completed in 1916 and included a palm house, two show houses and two plant houses. In 1954, the original Victorian conservatory was replaced by the present-day art-deco-styled conservatory. Renovated in 1997, the current conservatory is 10,000 square feet in size and houses a collection of tropical Amazon rain forest plants especially epiphytes and bromeliads. Hundreds of tropical and subtropical plants thrive in the glass house including arid plants, palms, orchids, ferns, *Theobroma cacao*, *Sapodilla chicle*, *Carica papaya*, *Musa banana*, *Coffea Arabica*, and *Citrus* species. Tropical free-flight birds such as zebra finches and green anole lizards and tree frogs may be seen amidst the plantings and about the 15-foot-high waterfall. Seasonal floral displays include a spring bulb show, a summer array of annuals, and a fall chrysanthemum show. A variety of plants are for sale in the gift shop.

In 1978, the Sunken Garden was restored and rededicated. Today's visitor may enjoy the three acres of European Classical formal gardens much as the visitors did in the early 1900s. The Sunken Garden's three historic and graceful fountains with their spouting geysers are surrounded by luxuriant plantings that include 10,000 spring tulips, daffodils and other bulbs, 1,000 pansies, 20,000 summer flowering plants and a variety of hardy mums in autumn. The 66 flower urns are reproductions of the originals. Benches provide sitting places along the paved pathways. Weddings and the concert series are frequently performed in the adjacent turf areas throughout the warmer months. Guided tours are available for a small fee if scheduled in advance.

*Garfield Park Conservatory & Sunken Garden, 2450 S. Shelby St. at 2505 Conservatory Dr., Indianapolis, IN 46203 **Tel:** (317) 327-7184 **Web:** www.garfieldgardensconservatory.org **Open:** Conservatory, daily, 10 a.m.-5 p.m.; Sunken Garden, daily, May 1-Oct. 15, 10 a.m.-10 p.m., Oct. 16-April 30 10 a.m.-5 p.m. **Acreage:** 4 conservatory & garden, 122 park **Fee(s):** admission to Conservatory, seasonal floral displays, workshops, facility rental, special events **Botanical Collections:** conservatory, rain forest, epiphytes, bromeliads, orchids, Victorian-styled sunken garden.

Garfield Park Conservatory, Indianapolis

Garfield Park Sunken Garden, Indianapolis

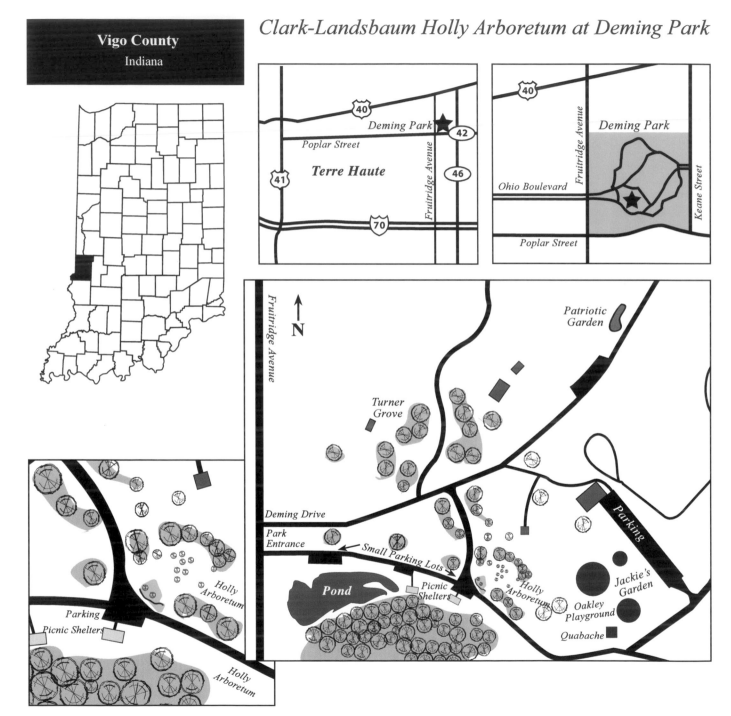

Clark-Landsbaum Holly Arboretum at Deming Park

Vigo County
Indiana

Terre Haute

Deming Park

Poplar Street

Fruitridge Avenue

40
41
42
46
70

Deming Park

Fruitridge Avenue

Ohio Boulevard

Keane Street

Poplar Street

N

Fruitridge Avenue

Patriotic Garden

Turner Grove

Deming Drive

Park Entrance

Small Parking Lots

Pond

Picnic Shelters

Holly Arboretum

Parking

Jackie's Garden

Oakley Playground

Quabache

Parking

Picnic Shelters

Holly Arboretum

Holly Arboretum

30. CLARK-LANDSBAUM HOLLY ARBORETUM AT DEMING PARK
TERRE HAUTE, INDIANA

Established in 1992, the Clark-Landsbaum Holly Arboretum at Deming Park is one of 18 Official U.S. Holly Arboretums designated by the Holly Society of America and one of 21 holly arboretums worldwide. The rare display of *Aquifoliaceae* or Holly Family members includes 435 woody plants representing 11 species of evergreen and deciduous trees and shrubs of the genus *Ilex*: *aquifolium* (English holly), *ciliospinosa*, *cornuta*, *crenata* (Japanese holly), *decidua*

(possumhaw), *glabra* (inkberry), *opaca* (American holly), *pedunculosa*, *serrata*, *verticillata* (winterberry or deciduous holly), and *vomitoria*. The excellent collection features 225 cultivars and more than 60 hybrid plants. The berries or drupes of holly may be colored red, orange, yellow, white or black, and only the female plant bears berries, but requires a male plant to do so (dioecious).

For easy identification each plant is labeled. There are two bluestone patios and benches where visitors may sit and view the arboretum from a vantage point along the south-facing hill slope. Special projects and events are held on occasion to draw attention to the arboretum and guided tours may be scheduled. The

Entrance Sign, Clark-Landsbaum Holly Arboretum, Terre Haute

Friends of the Arboretum, a non-profit volunteer organization, in cooperation with the Terre Haute Parks Department, have developed and are maintaining the award-winning arboretum.

To reach the holly arboretum from Fruitridge Avenue in east Terre Haute, enter Deming Park at the Ohio Boulevard west park entrance. Watch for the holly arboretum sign at the intersection of the first park crossover road. Parking is available in the picnic shelter lots just past Front Pond.

> *"That in my age as cheerful I might be,*
> *As the green winter of the Holly Tree."*
> **Robert Southey**

*Clark-Landsbaum Holly Arboretum at Deming Park, (located just west of Dobbs Park), 500 S. Fruitridge Ave. at Poplar St., Terre Haute, IN 47803 **Tel:** (812) 232-2727, 877-1087 **Web:** www.demingparkhollyarboretum.com **Open:** daily, dawn to dusk **Acreage:** 8 arboretum, 177 park **Fee(s):** donations & gifts accepted **Botanical Collections:** official holly arboretum.

Irwin Garden

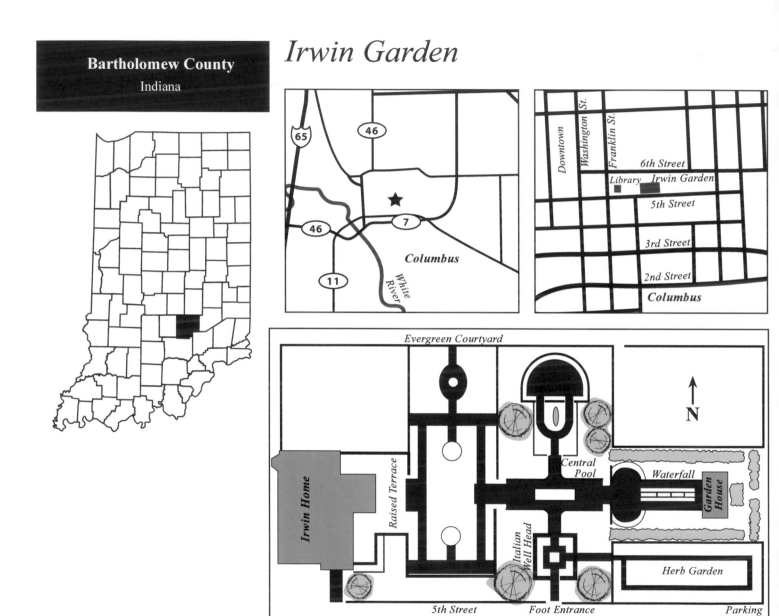

Bartholomew County
Indiana

65
46
46
7
11
Columbus
White River

Downtown
Washington St.
Franklin St.
6th Street
Library   Irwin Garden
5th Street
3rd Street
2nd Street
Columbus

Evergreen Courtyard

N

Irwin Home

Raised Terrace

Central Pool

Waterfall

Garden House

Italian Well Head

Herb Garden

5th Street   Foot Entrance   Parking

> *"He who has a garden and a library wants for nothing."*
> **Marcus Tullius Cicero**

The Irwin family's Italianate-styled home had its beginnings in 1864, but was renovated in 1884, and redesigned and enlarged in 1910 by Massachusetts architect, Henry A. Phillips. The adjoining Italian-styled gardens, designed after an ancient Roman estate garden in suburban Pompeii, were added by Phillips to the east of the house and completed in 1911; however, several garden elements were incorporated since the original design. From the time the gardens have been installed, it has been the family tradition and joy to open the garden to visitors on weekends from mid-April to mid-October.

The one-acre Irwin estate garden is comprised of eight interconnecting areas accessible along brick and flagstone pathways. Connecting the home to the gardens is a raised terrace with covered areas at the north and south ends. Below the terrace on the upper garden level are two open wisteria-covered pergolas positioned on both ends of the grass-covered courtyard. Four statues of Greek philosophers, reproductions from the gardens of Emperor Hadrian's villa at Tivoli, appear along the walls: Socrates, Diogenes, Plato and Aristotle. Along the north pergola, a pathway leads to the Evergreen Courtyard where a Florentine Crane statue towers over a bird bath bordered by evergreen shrubs.

From the upper garden level, steps descend to the Central Pool and Sunken Garden. To the north of the Central Pool is a bronze elephant statue with steps leading above to an elevated semi-circular brick wall reminiscent of an Italian Renaissance garden feature. To the south of the Central Pool is the Medieval Italian well-head and the 5th Street main garden gated entrance beyond. To the east of the Medieval Italian well, a pathway leads to a gate and the enclosed English Knot Garden that features over 1,000 culinary and medicinal plants. Perhaps the most spectacular area is the elevated Roman-Pompeian garden summer house and fountain waterfall that overlooks the garden and house.

Sunken Garden, Irwin Garden, Columbus

Although floral greenery is an important element in an Italian garden, some of the flowering plants include pansies, flowering spring bulbs, impatiens, begonia, petunia, vinca, asters, sedum and chrysanthemums. Many annuals are grown in the 7,500-foot square greenhouse northwest of the garden. Additional plants include European linden, Bradford pear, Norway spruce, Japanese yew, buddleia, boxwood and ivy. Throughout the lavish formal garden are several fountains, statuary, sculptures, planter vases, a sundial, murals, gates, a fountain waterfall and benches.

*Irwin Garden, (located just east of the public library), 608 5th St., Columbus, IN 47201 **Tel:** (812) 376-3331 **Web:** www.columbus.in.us **Open:** Sat.- Sun, 8 a.m.- 4 p.m. **Acreage:** less than one **Fee(s):** none **Botanical Collections:** Italian-style garden, English herb garden, fountains, statuary.

T. C. Steele Gardens & Grounds

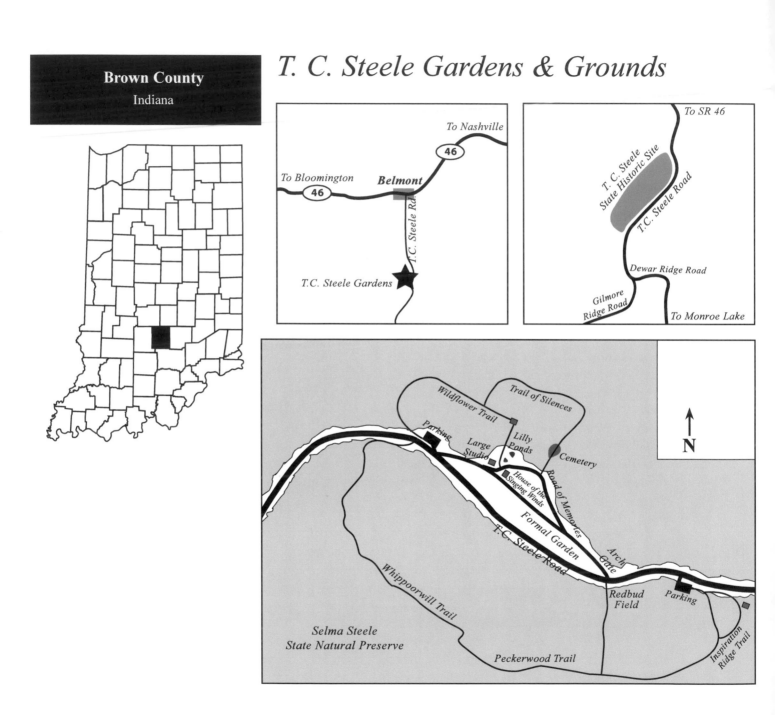

Brown County
Indiana

To Nashville
46
To Bloomington
Belmont
46
T.C. Steele Rd.
T.C. Steele Gardens

To SR 46
T. C. Steele State Historic Site
T.C. Steele Road
Dewar Ridge Road
Gilmore Ridge Road
To Monroe Lake

Wildflower Trail
Trail of Silences
Parking
Large Studio
Lilly Ponds
Cemetery
House of the Singing Winds
Road of Memories
Formal Garden
Arch Gate
T.C. Steele Road
Redbud Field
Parking
Whippoorwill Trail
Selma Steele State Natural Preserve
Peckerwood Trail
Inspiration Ridge Trail
N

32. T. C. Steele Gardens & Grounds
Belmont, Indiana

> "Nature showed me her way
> of growing things."
>
> **Selma Steele**

In April 1907, Theodore Clement Steele (1845-1926), impressionist painter, and his second wife, Selma Neubacher Steele (1870-1945), purchased the abandoned Bracken Hill Farm near Belmont, Indiana, in western Brown County. After 60 years of living, studying and painting in places such as Waveland, Gosport, Brookville and Indianapolis, Indiana; Chicago, Illinois; and Munich, Germany, Steele moved to the "House of the Singing Winds" he had built during the summer of 1907 for his new wife. The landscaping was largely designed and developed by Selma Steele and her labor was often the subject and inspiration for her husband's paintings.

In 1908, the first work of permanent landscaping were flower beds and paths, the same year the house was doubled in size. Over the years that followed, Mrs. Steele created several acres of delicate gardens, enhancing the beauty of the woodland scene that served as a background to the garden picture. To the neighbors, it was an "inexcusable waste of money and labor to grow flowers."

Blooming by the thousands, flowering bulbs such as daffodils and jonquils covered the hillsides "in the soft atmosphere of springtime." In 1913, one acre was planted in orchard, another hillside was planted in small fruits such as grapes and strawberries, and over 600 evergreens were planted. Despite the difficulties of establishing a landscape of "elusive beauty" where the ridge top soil was thin and poor for gardening, Selma's main joy was realizing she had made "the flower and garden arrangements interesting enough to be placed on the painter's canvases."

Since 1945, the Steele property has been administered as an Indiana Department of Natural Resources site "to inspire future art and nature lovers." Pre-arranged guided garden tours are offered; however, visitors are welcome to stroll through Mrs. Steele's restored gardens. Guided tours of the home and the barn studio where numerous paintings are displayed are also offered. In addition, the Dewar log cabin serves as a nature center. The historic site also includes five hiking trails and the 92-acre Selma N. Steele State Nature Preserve. The "Wildflower Foray" is a special late April event.

*T. C. Steele State Historic Site, (located between Nashville and Bloomington), 4220 T. C. Steele Rd., Nashville, IN 47448 **Tel:** (812) 988-2785 **Web:** www.tcsteele.org **Open:** year round, seasonal hours may vary Tues.-Sat., 9 a.m.-5 p.m., Sun., 1 p.m.-5 p.m., closed Monday & legal holidays, open July 4th & Labor Day **Acreage:** 3 gardens, 15 house and grounds, 211 total **Fee(s):** gardens & grounds free, admission for home & studio tour **Botanical Collections:** historic house gardens, wildflowers.

Peonies in May Bloom, T. C. Steele Gardens, Belmont

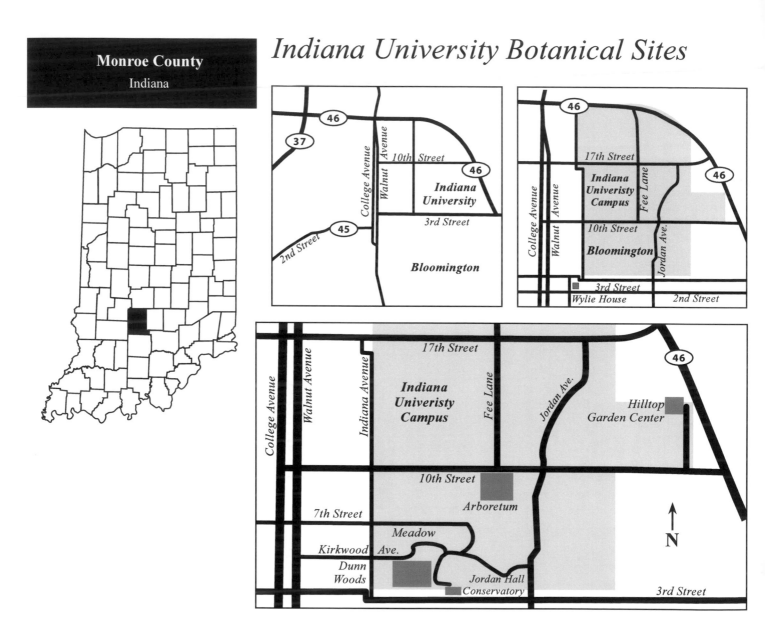

Indiana University Botanical Sites

Monroe County
Indiana

46
37
45
2nd Street
College Avenue
Walnut Avenue
10th Street
46
Indiana University
3rd Street
Bloomington

46
College Avenue
Walnut Avenue
17th Street
Indiana Univeristy Campus
Fee Lane
46
10th Street
Bloomington
Jordan Ave.
3rd Street
Wylie House
2nd Street

17th Street
College Avenue
Walnut Avenue
Indiana Avenue
Indiana Univeristy Campus
Fee Lane
Jordan Ave.
46
Hilltop Garden Center
10th Street
Arboretum
7th Street
Meadow Ave.
Kirkwood Ave.
Dunn Woods
Jordan Hall Conservatory
3rd Street
N

33. INDIANA UNIVERSITY BOTANICAL SITES
BLOOMINGTON, INDIANA

The campus of Indiana University is one of the most beautiful campuses in the Midwest, if not the nation. Once open farm fields, the entire Bloomington campus, over 2,000 acres, has thousands of trees, shrubs and flowers and may be considered a botanic garden; however, the main botanical resources of the central campus are the Hoosier Arboretum, Jordan Hall Greenhouse, Hilltop Garden and Nature Center, and the Wylie House Museum and Heirloom Gardens.

The 20-acre arboretum, located between the Herman Wells Main Library and Woodlawn Field along East 10th Street at Fee Lane, occupies the site where the former Memorial Stadium once stood. From seven entry points, all-weather paths

Flowering Kousa Dogwoods,
Indiana University Arboretum, Bloomington

crisscross the arboretum. A pond lies at the arboretum center constantly supplied by a cascading fountain stream descending from the upland gazebo. The grounds are planted with 450 labeled native and exotic woody plants and hundreds of varieties of flowers. Special collections include the plant family members of the *Aceraceae* (maple), *Juglandaceae* (walnut), *Pinaceae* (pine), *Rosaceae* (rose), *Cornaceae* (dogwood) and *Aquifoliaceae* (holly) families. Indiana alumni, Jesse H. and Beulah C. Cox, benefactors of Carmel, Indiana's Coxhall Gardens, donated generously to the development of the arboretum. The arboretum is open year-around.

The Jordan Hall Greenhouse is located at the corner of 1001 East Third Street and Hawthorne Drive. The biology department grows plants that serve the teaching and research needs of the faculty and students. Visitors are welcome to stop in the conservatory to view the mostly exotic tropical rainforest and desert plant life. A self-guiding tour brochure is available and group tours may be arranged.

> *"We believe there is a strong tie between academic excellence and aesthetic quality of the surroundings."*
> **Terry Clapaces**

Since 1948, Hilltop Garden and Nature Center remains one of the oldest children's gardening centers in the nation, (the Brooklyn Botanical Gardens is the oldest children's gardening program). The mission of the university facility is to provide a central place for research and education in gardening and nature. Operated by the Department of Recreation, Park and Tourism Studies,

Hilltop's five acres contains 75 organic, children- planted tree and vegetable plots, fruits trees, a seasonal tropical garden, flower and herb gardens, special display plantings, greenhouse, classroom, library and test gardens.

Hilltop Garden and Nature Center is located just west of the SR 45/46 Bypass at 2367 E. 10th Street. From the Bypass and E. 10th Street intersection, take the first driveway west adjacent to the Tulip Tree Apartment high rise and drive to the dead end parking and garden entrance. Call ahead for tours.

Southwest of campus a few blocks is the Wylie House Museum, the 1835 home and gardens of the first president of Indiana University. An outdoor interpreter is in charge of planning and overseeing the gardens where pre-1859 heirloom flower, vegetable and herb varieties are cultivated. The garden's antique grapevines and roses were planted during the Civil War (1861-1865). Heirloom seeds collected from the Wylie House gardens may be purchased at the gift shop. Guided tours of the home and gardens are offered from March through November, Tuesday-Saturday, 10 a.m. to 2 p.m. or by arrangement. The location of the Wylie House Museum is at the northeast corner of the 2nd Street and Lincoln Street at 307 E. 2nd Street.

*Jordan Hall Conservatory,
Indiana University, Bloomington*

Additional campus green areas include Dunn Woods and Meadow, Woodlawn Field and Bryan House grounds.

Indiana University, (bordered by Dunn St., Atwater Ave., & the SR 45/46 Bypass), Visitor Information Carmichael Center, 530 E. Kirkwood Ave, Suite 104, Bloomington, IN 47408 **Tel**: (812) 856-4648 **Web**: www.indiana.edu/~iuvis **Open**: arboretum, daily, dawn to dusk; Jordan Hall greenhouse, Mon.-Fri., 7:30 a.m.- 4 p.m., Sat. & Sun., 9 a.m.-3 p.m.; Hilltop Garden & Nature Center, Mon.-Sat., 9 a.m.-5 p.m., closed Sunday & holidays; Wylie House Museum, grounds open daily **Acreage**: arboretum 20; Jordan Hall greenhouse less than one; Hilltop Garden & Nature Center 5; Wylie House Museum 1.5 **Fee(s)**: facility & garden plot rental, classes, workshops at Hilltop Gardens & Nature Center **Botanical Collections**: arboretum, tropical & subtropical greenhouses, flower, herb, vegetable, seasonal tropical & heirloom gardens.

Tropical Garden, Hilltop Garden, Indiana University, Bloomington

Spring Mill Pioneer Village Gardens

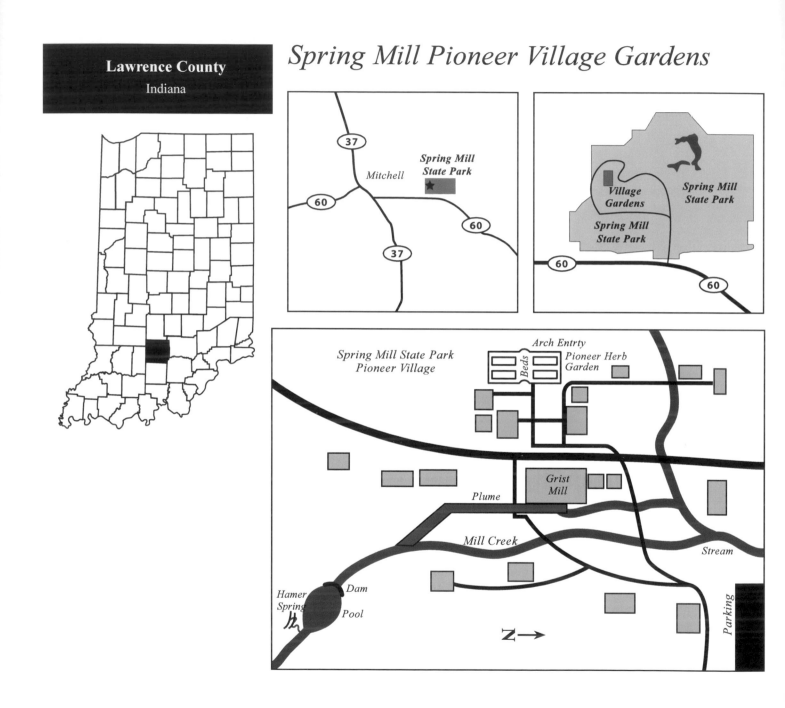

Lawrence County
Indiana

Spring Mill State Park

Mitchell

Spring Mill
State Park

Village
Gardens

Spring Mill
State Park

Spring Mill
State Park

Spring Mill State Park
Pioneer Village

Arch Entrty

Beds

Pioneer Herb
Garden

Grist
Mill

Plume

Mill Creek

Stream

Hamer
Spring

Dam

Pool

Parking

N→

34. SPRING MILL PIONEER VILLAGE GARDEN
MITCHELL, INDIANA

> "To cultivate a garden is to walk with God."
>
> **Christian N. Bovee**

When Spring Mill State Park was established in 1927, the main focus was the authentic re-creation of the 1800s-era pioneer village of Spring Mill (est. 1814). Due to these earlier reconstructive efforts dating to the 1930s, today's visitor may stroll through and tour the restored pioneer "living history" village of Spring Mill where time has seemingly stood still. In order to immerse visitors in early Indiana pioneer days, historical interpreters dressed in period costumes are on hand from May through October to demonstrate the crafts and chores of the former villagers.

Located at the west edge of the village and on the site of the original garden established by the Hamer brothers are the restored pioneer gardens that display nearly 150 native and exotic varieties of heirloom flowers and herbs that were cultivated and utilized by the Hoosier pioneers prior to the Civil War. A large number of the garden plants were gathered from former homesteads and from the wilds within the 1,358 acre state park.

The gardens are enclosed by low native limestone walls and arched entry ways mark the main entrance. The rectangular-shaped formal beds overflow with a vast array of labeled ornamental, fragrant, culinary, and medicinal plants that collectively are at their blooming best in June and July.

An excellent carefully-researched guidebook entitled *Flower and Herbs in the Pioneer Village Gardens* is available for purchase. The Heirloom Plant and Seed Exchange event is held each spring at the gardens, usually in April. The combination of history, horticulture and scenery makes Spring Mill village a special botanic outing.

Spring Mill State Park is located 3.5 miles east of Mitchell, Indiana, and the intersection of S.R. 37 on S.R. 60. Additional pioneer gardens are featured at Brown County State Park and O'Bannon Wood State Park adjacent to the nature centers.

*Spring Mill State Park, 3333 S.R. 60 E., Mitchell, IN 47446 **Tel:** (812) 849-4129 **Web:** www.dnr.IN.gov/parklake **Open:** daily, late spring, early summer is best time for viewing gardens **Acreage:** less than one acre gardens, ten acre pioneer village, 1,358 acre park **Fee(s):** park admission **Botanical Collections:** restored pioneer gardens, heirloom flowers & herbs.

Garden Entrance, Pioneer Village Garden, Spring Mill State Park, Mitchell

West Baden Springs Sunken Garden

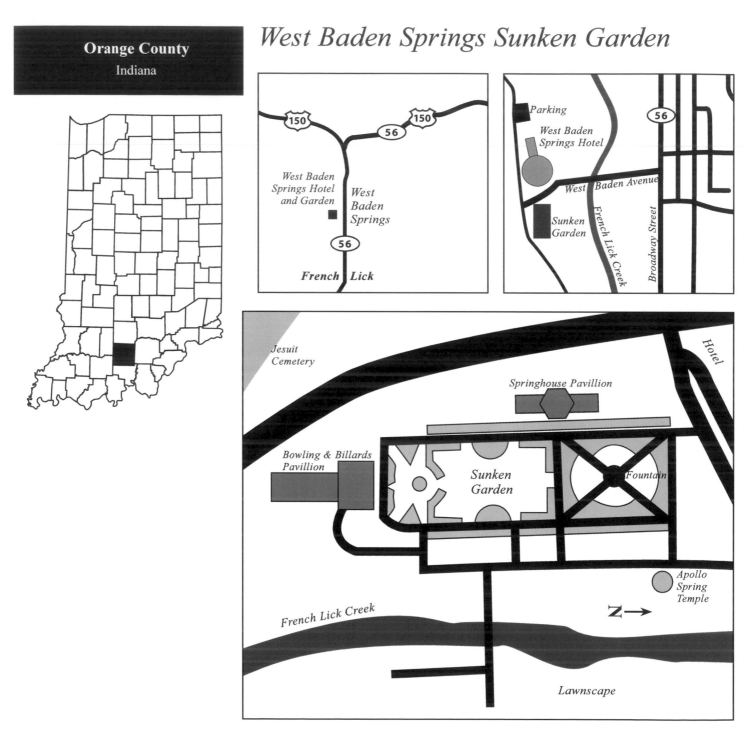

Orange County
Indiana

150 56 150

West Baden
Springs Hotel
and Garden

West
Baden
Springs

56

French Lick

Parking

56

West Baden
Springs Hotel

West Baden Avenue

Sunken
Garden

French Lick Creek

Broadway Street

Jesuit
Cemetery

Hotel

Springhouse Pavillion

Bowling & Billards
Pavillion

Sunken
Garden

Fountain

Apollo
Spring
Temple

N→

French Lick Creek

Lawnscape

35. WEST BADEN SPRINGS SUNKEN GARDEN
WEST BADEN, INDIANA

Established in 1917, the formal Italianate-styled sunken garden was installed to complement the West Baden Springs Hotel, "the Eighth Wonder of the World" and the "Carlsbad of America." Based on historic photographs, the gardens were restored in 1997-1998 after several years of neglect. The size of a football field, the three-acre Greco-Roman themed gardens were edged by three former springs pavilions, whose waters were once known for their medicinal and curative properties, and a billards and bowling pavilion. A fourth spring pavilion, Neptune Spring, was situated 100 yards east of the sunken garden, connected by a pedestrian bridge over French Lick Creek and an oak allee.

Sunken Garden, West Baden Springs Hotel, West Baden Springs

Situated to the south of the hotel and driveway, the gardens may be accessed through the two entry pergolas. Brick pathways lead to the fountain, the focal point of the gardens. Many annual and perennial beds grace the rectangular-shaped sunken garden, including peonies, pansies, daffodils, lilies, chrysanthemums and herbal beds of thyme. Boxwood frames the formal flowerbed parterres. Columns of arborvitae surround the central mall and specimen trees and shrubs of flowering magnolia, crabapple, dogwood, cherry and viburnums are scattered about the garden's edges. Evergreen of spruce and hemlock form the outermost borders.

The garden is flanked on three sides by historic structures: Hygeia Spring pavilion is on the west, the Billards and Bowling Pavilion is on the south, and Apollo Spring is on the northeast. Sprudel Spring pavilion and the Neptune Spring pavilion have long been removed.

The gardens are at their peak in June through August. Visitors may park their vehicles in the parking area to the north of the hotel and enjoy the park-like grounds. Fee-guided tours of the gardens and hotel are available from Historic Landmarks Foundation of Indiana at the Landmarks Emporium within the hotel.

> *"There is always music amongst the trees in the garden, but one's heart must be very quiet to hear it."*
> **Minnie Aumonier**

*****West Baden Springs Hotel & Gardens**, (one mile north of French Lick), 8538 West Baden Ave., S.R. 56, West Baden Springs, IN 47469 **Tel:** (800) 450-4534, (812) 936-1902, (877) 561-8687 **Web:** www.historiclandmarks. org or www.frenchlick.org **Open:** daily, daylight hours **Acreage:** gardens 3 **Fee(s):** guided tours daily, 10 a.m., 12 p.m., 2 p.m. & 4 p.m. **Botanical Collections:** formal Italianate sunken garden.

Stream Cliff Herb Farm

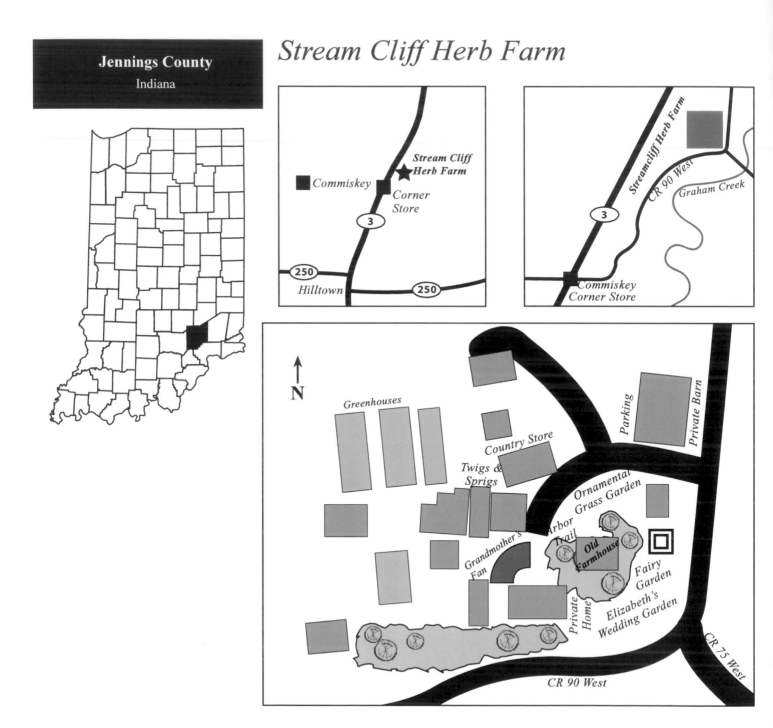

Jennings County
Indiana

Commiskey

Corner Store

Stream Cliff Herb Farm

3

250

250

Hilltown

Streamcliff Herb Farm

CR 90 West

Graham Creek

3

Commiskey Corner Store

N

Greenhouses

Country Store

Twigs & Sprigs

Parking

Private Barn

Ornamental Grass Garden

Arbor Trail

Grandmother's Fan

Old Farmhouse

Fairy Garden

Private Home

Elizabeth's Wedding Garden

CR 75 West

CR 90 West

36. STREAM CLIFF HERB FARM
COMMISKEY, INDIANA

Located high and dry above Big Graham Creek, Stream Cliff Herb Farm was first homesteaded in 1821, and since the early 1900s, after a century of family ownership, it is now the family farm of Betty and Gerald Manning. The Mannings have been involved in the herb business since the 1970s and their children, the fifth generation to live on the historic farmstead, are also involved in the family herbal enterprise. Billed as "Indiana's oldest herb farm," Stream Cliff's uniqueness has caught the attention of several national magazines. Articles about the herb farm have appeared in *Beautiful Gardens*, *Midwest Living*, *Garden Shed*, *Gardening How-To*, and *Herb Companion*.

The various quilt-block-shaped thematic gardens are dedicated to Betty's Manning's grandmother, Luella Tate Artz, who was an avid quilter and gardener and resided for more than 50 years on the farm. Some of the garden's themes and styles, several with water features, include Grandmother's Fan Gardens, Dresden Plate, Fairy Garden, Bridal Garden, Crucifix Garden, Sanctuary Garden, Butterfly Garden, Children's Garden and Ornamental Grass Garden. There is also a Bluebird

Home & Garden, Stream Cliff Herb Farm, Commiskey

Arbor Trail. Hundreds of varieties, some difficult to find, of herbs, perennial flowers, everlastings, old-fashioned roses, and butterfly bushes are for sale.

> *"This is a very spiritual place, a place to give your self time to look around and find beauty in nature."*
> **Betty Manning**

In addition to the lovely display gardens are four unique garden and craft shops where visitors may purchase garden accessories and books and handmade crafts; a delightful Twigs and Sprigs Tearoom which features an herbal luncheon menu and afternoon tea; plus a winery are located at the farm. Additional amenities include group tour packages, classes, workshops, dinner reservations and special events.

Historic Stream Cliff Herb Farm is located 0.5 miles east of S.R. 3 on Commiskey Road (the road opposite of the Commiskey Corner Store) in southern Jennings County.

*Stream Cliff Herb Farm, 8225 S C.R. 90 W, Commiskey, IN 47227   Tel: (812) 346-5859   Web: www.streamclifffarm.com   Open: April-October, Wed.-Sat., 10 a.m.-4 p.m., Sunday, noon - 4 p.m., closed Mondays & Tuesday and holidays   Acreage: 2 gardens, farm 470   Fee(s): group tour packages, classes, workshops   Botanical Collections: quilt-styled herb gardens, thematic gardens.

Cathedral Gardens

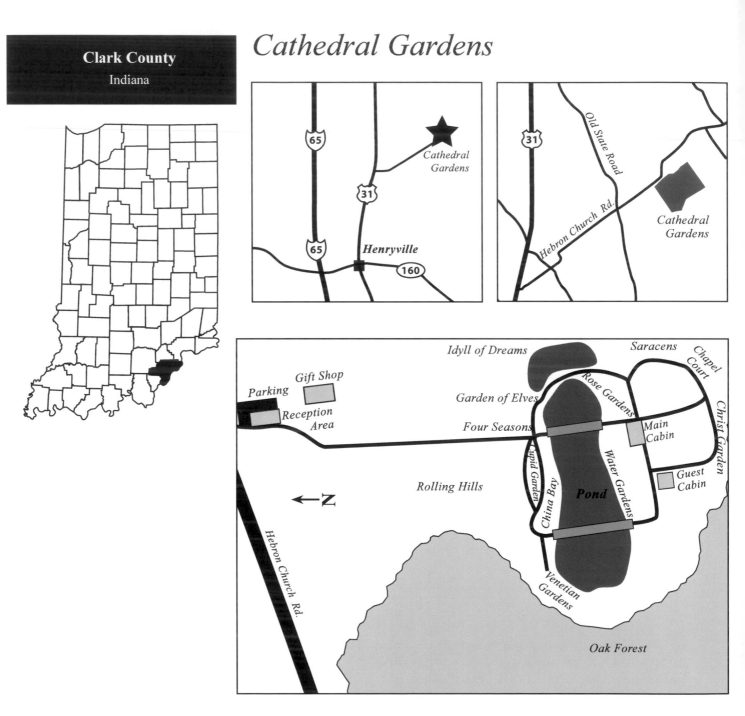

Clark County
Indiana

65
31
Cathedral Gardens
65
31
Henryville
160

31
Old State Road
Hebron Church Rd.
Cathedral Gardens

Idyll of Dreams
Saracens
Chapel Court
Gift Shop
Garden of Elves
Rose Gardens
Parking
Reception Area
Four Seasons
Main Cabin
Christ Garden
Cupid Garden
Water Gardens
Guest Cabin
Rolling Hills
China Bay
Pond
N
Hebron Church Rd.
Venetian Gardens

Oak Forest

37. CATHEDRAL GARDENS
HENRYVILLE, INDIANA

Cathedral Gardens, a private spiritual retreat, was first opened to the public in 2003 after a decade of design and development by David L. Daugherty. The mission of this fanciful place is the "enrichment of spiritual and creative thought and quest of paradise."

Fifteen acres within the 52-acre property contain twelve thematic gardens that are decorated with extensive plantings, scenic lakes, opulent fountains, stylish pavilions and imported statuary, vases and urns. The twelve distinctive gardens include the Brownstone Garden, Chapel Court, China Bay, Christ's Garden, Cupid Garden, Four Season's Garden, Garden of Elves, Greek Garden, Rose Garden, Saracen's Retreat Garden, Venetian Garden, and the Water Garden. Tens of thousands of flowering annuals and perennials as well as flowering trees and shrubs grace the grounds of this floral setting that strives to be an elegant example of heaven on earth.

Christ's Garden, Cathedral Gardens, Henryville

Two-hour personalized garden tours are guided by staff members four times daily, except Sunday which is by appointment. Special tours may be scheduled in advance. Guests may tour in wagons, van or golf cart depending on personal needs and guests are welcome to remain throughout the day. Picnicking is permitted. Facility rental is available for weddings or private parties. Plants, artwork and crafts are available for purchase in the gift shop.

Cathedral Gardens is located north and east of Henryville and I-65 and U.S. 31 about 2.5 miles on Hebron Church Road.

> *"We strive to give our guests a panoramic gift which they can forever keep as inspiration for a more beautiful, peaceful world in tribute to the Creator."*
> **David L. Daugherty**

*Cathedral Gardens, (30 minutes north of Louisville, KY, 10 miles south of Scottsburg), 1314 Hebron Church Rd., Henryville, IN 47126   **Tel:** (812) 294-3193 **Web:** www.cathedralgardens.com   **Open:** May through October, 8 a.m.-5 p.m., personalized tours four times daily, 9 a.m., 11 a.m., 1 p.m. & 3 p.m., Sunday by appt. **Acreage:** 15 gardens, 52 total **Fee(s):** admission, facility rental **Botanical Collections:** formal thematic gardens, historic & international garden styles, water gardens, sculpture.

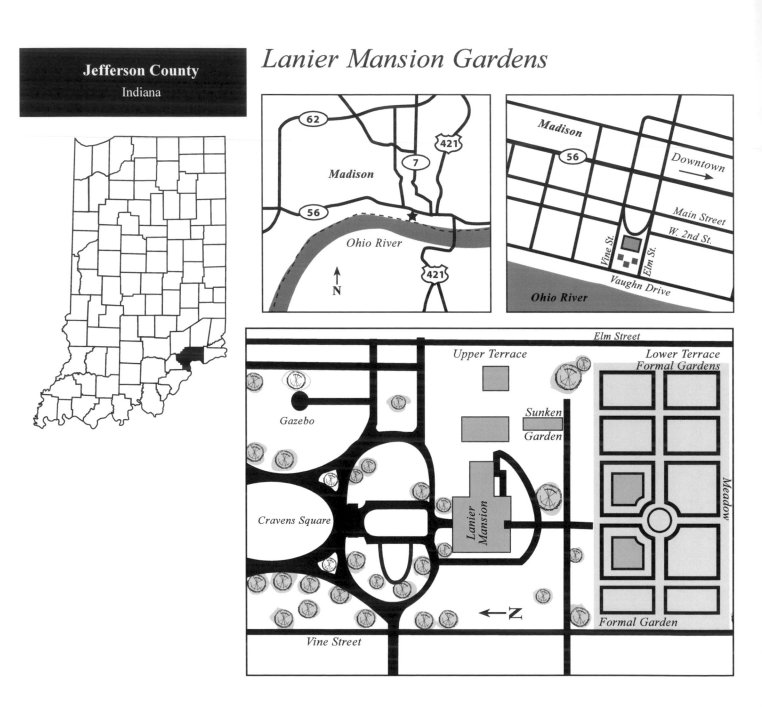

Lanier Mansion Gardens

Jefferson County
Indiana

62

421

7

Madison

56

Ohio River

N

421

Madison

56

Downtown

Main Street

Vine St.

Elm St.

W. 2nd St.

Vaughn Drive

Ohio River

Elm Street

Upper Terrace

Lower Terrace
Formal Gardens

Sunken
Garden

Gazebo

Meadow

Cravens Square

Lanier
Mansion

N

Formal Garden

Vine Street

38. LANIER MANSION GARDENS & GROUNDS
MADISON, INDIANA

> *"He who plants a garden plants happiness."*
> **Proverb**

Since 1925, the 1844 Greek Revival home of financier, James Franklin Doughty Lanier has been a state historic site. Lanier was a builder of Indiana's banking institutions and railroads and during the Civil War he supported the northern war effort through loans to the state. Four generations of Lanier's resided in the three-story eight-bedroom home prior to it being donated in the early twentieth century as a historic site by his youngest son, Charles. Today, the Lanier Mansion, Indiana's first state historic site is also a National Historic Landmark.

The landscape history of the grounds encompassing the mansion during the years of J. F. D. Lanier's residency (1844-1851) remains a mystery; however, after the Civil War, Lanier's oldest son, Alexander, an avid horticulturalist developed the gardens and grounds, constructing several stately greenhouses. Unfortunately, after Alexander's death in 1895, the impressive floral array was neglected and eventually abandoned, and later covered with a foot-thick layer of river silt from flooding. Fortunately, the aesthetic splendor of the late 19th century grounds is revealed in a well preserved 1876 lithograph. The historic recreation of the post-Civil War landscape is based on the 1876 image that evokes the romantic graciousness of the era.

Today the elegant and historic landscape consists of four areas: Cravens Square, Upper Terrace, Lower Terrace and Pasture. Cravens Square, the north yard facing West Second Street, is actually donated land (1944), and not part of the original property. Magnolias, weeping cherries, Kousa dogwoods, lilacs, roses, spring flowering bulbs and annuals thrive alongside the curving walks. The Upper Terrace, from Vine to Elm streets and facing the Ohio River, features a walled sunken garden constructed in 1928. Wildflowers, herbs, perennials, annuals, roses, spirea, rose of Sharon, and yucca provide a colorful texture tapestry. The Lower Terrace directly in front of the mansion's south façade displays the recreated formal garden's grandeur. There are ten geometric-shaped beds or parterres enclosed by hedges of boxwood. Heirloom flowers, vines, dwarf fruit trees, shrub and planting occupy the beds. Gravel paths provide up close foot access.

Beyond the formal gardens lies the grassy lawn pasture with bold sweeping views of the Ohio River and Kentucky.

Additional gardens to visit while in Madison include the Talbot-Hyatt Pioneer Garden at 301 W. 2nd Street; Dr. Wm. Hutchings herb garden at 120 W. Third Street; and the Lanthier Winery's "Gardens of Art" at 123 Mill Street.

*Lanier Mansion State Historic Site, 601 W. First St., Madison, IN 47250 **Tel:** (812) 265-3526 **Web:** www.indianamuseum.org **Open:** daily, grounds dawn to dusk **Acreage:** 10 **Fee(s):** mansion tour, facility rental, special events **Botanical Collections:** historic estate formal gardens, sunken garden, cutting gardens.

Formal Gardens, Lower Terrace, Lanier Mansion Gardens, Madison

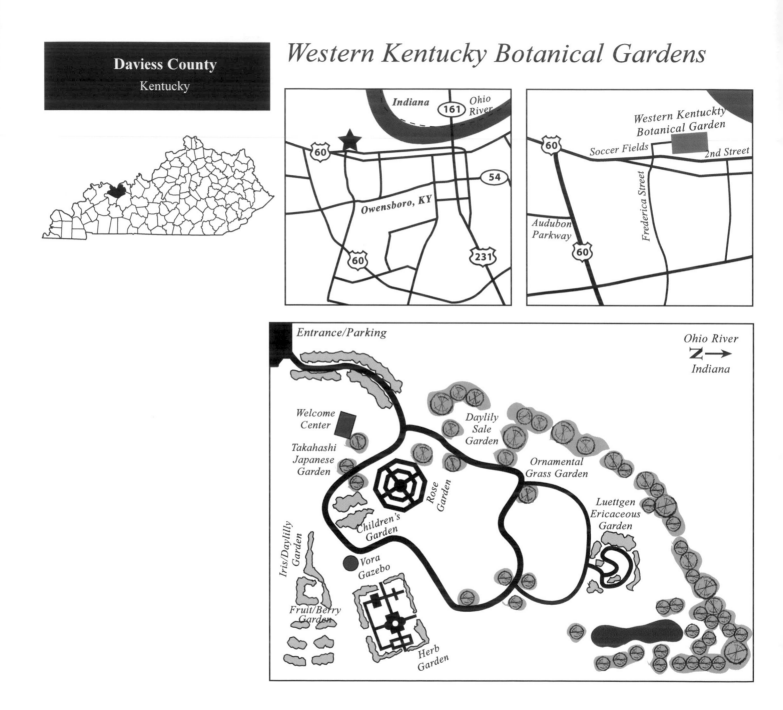

Western Kentucky Botanical Gardens

Daviess County
Kentucky

Indiana
Ohio River
161
60
54
Owensboro, KY
60
231

Western Kentuckty Botanical Garden
60
Soccer Fields
2nd Street
Frederica Street
Audubon Parkway
60

Entrance/Parking

Ohio River
N→
Indiana

Welcome Center
Takahashi Japanese Garden
Daylily Sale Garden
Ornamental Grass Garden
Rose Garden
Children's Garden
Luettgen Ericaceous Garden
Iris/Daylily Garden
Vora Gazebo
Fruit/Berry Garden
Herb Garden

OTANICAL GARDEN
ENSBORO, KENTUCKY

boro's west end is the charming
botanic site, whose objective is
dedicated volunteers, relying
r of visual-rich gardens and
which makes visiting a perfect

ng to different themes and made
a miniature nature landscape, is

hybrid teas, English and old-
eral theme gardens such as a
in The Garden.

ion of medicinal, tea, culinary,
storic Country Doctor's Office
aylily gardens and a Fruit and

and the picturesque Luettgen
Garden includes ten different

Colonel Sanders Ash, Kremlin Ash, Johnny Appleseed Apple, Ming Dynasty Cypress, Issac Newton Apple and Casey Jones Willow Oak complete the overall garden image.

Guided tours are available and educational programs, plant sales and special events are held year around. There is a horticultural library located in the Welcome Center. Planned future gardens include a Developmentally Disabled Garden, an English Cottage Garden, Native Plant Garden, Shade Garden, a Pinetum plus an amphitheatre.

Rose Garden, Western Kentucky Botanical Garden, Owensboro, Kentucky

*Western Kentucky Botanic Garden, 2nd Street at N. Carter Rd., P. O. Box 22562, Owensboro, KY 42304 Tel: (270) 852-8925 Web: www.wkbg.org Open: daily, sunrise to sunset, Welcome Center hours 9 a.m.-3 p.m., Monday-Friday Acreage: 9 Fee(s): donations accepted, facility rental, educational programs, special events, garden membership Botanical Collections: Japanese Garden, formal rose garden, children's garden, herb garden, peonies, iris, daylilies, azaleas, rhododendrons, ornamental grasses, annuals, historic trees.

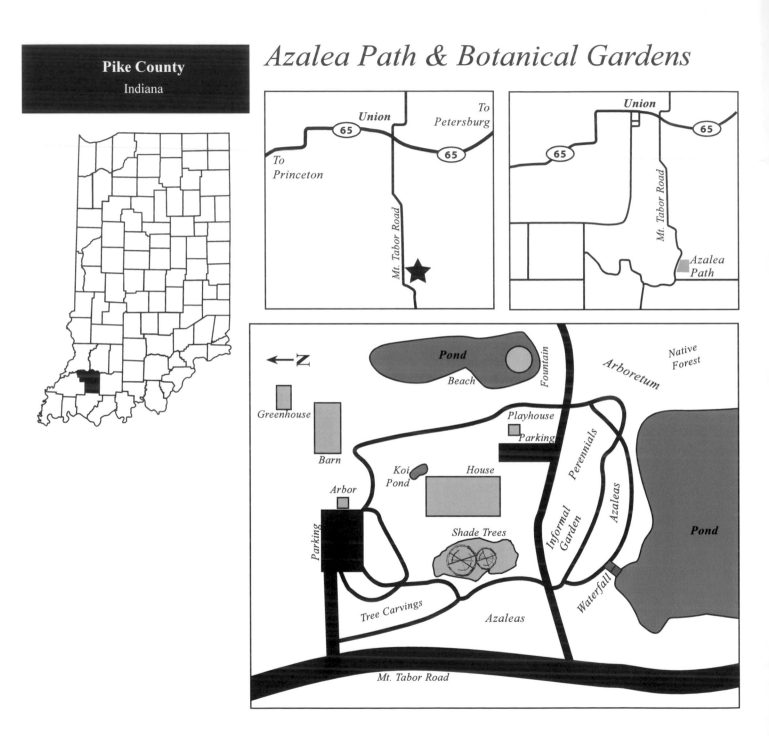

Azalea Path & Botanical Gardens

Pike County
Indiana

Union
65
To Petersburg
To Princeton
65
Mt. Tabor Road

Union
65
65
Mt. Tabor Road
Azalea Path

Pond
Beach
Fountain
Native Forest
Arboretum
N
Greenhouse
Barn
Playhouse
Parking
Koi Pond
House
Perennials
Arbor
Parking
Shade Trees
Informal Garden
Azaleas
Pond
Tree Carvings
Azaleas
Waterfall
Mt. Tabor Road

40. AZALEA PATH ARBORETUM & BOTANICAL GARDEN
PRINCETON, INDIANA

These nonprofit and privately-owned gardens were inspired by Dr. H. H. Schroeder, an internationally renowned azalea hybridizer whose scientific focus was on developing colorful and hardy azalea varieties for northern climes. Nearly all of the varieties Dr. Schroeder developed are displayed at Azalea Path, a 15-acre botanic site that had its beginnings in 1979.

> *"Gardening is a way of showing that you believe in tomorrow."*
>
> **Anonymous**

Thirty years after the first planting by Mrs. Knight, the gardens have undergone a dramatic change. Wood-chipped paths now weave through delicate woodland scenes that include 300 varieties of azaleas, nearly 2,000 shrubs that thrive in the shady understory, sunny openings and along the open lakeshore. For those who love azaleas and floral beauty, consider a springtime visit to the appropriately-named Azalea Path Arboretum and Botanical Garden.

In addition to the unique azalea collection that provides spectacular and stunning blazes of May color, visitors also marvel at the variety of unusual trees and shrubs from Europe and Asia. Native and exotic shade and flowering trees dot the garden landscape. Dogwood and redbud, rhododendron and lilac are also in flower when the azaleas bring forth their radiant display.

Water elements also play an important role in the gardens and include two spring-fed lakes, a rushing waterfall, koi pond and several fountains. Sizeable boulders are scattered among the plantings. Numerous sculptures, statuary and arbors are also featured. A storm-battered pine grove showcases several animal-sculptured tree stump carvings by chainsaw artist, James Taylor. The lovely pleasure garden is a rewarding place to visit not only in spring, but also summer and fall.

*Garden Entrance,
Azalea Path Arboretum & Botanical Garden, Union*

Straddling the Gibson-Pike county line, Azalea Path is located in the country, south three miles from the village of Union, 14 miles northeast of Princeton, Indiana.

*Azalea Path Arboretum & Botanical Gardens, 1502 N. C.R. 825 W., Hazleton, IN 47640-9507 **Tel:** (812) 354-3039 **Web:** www.gibsoncountyin.org/attractions **Open:** daily, dawn to dusk, April thru October **Acreage:** 15 gardens, 50 total **Fee(s):**donations accepted **Botanical Collections:** azaleas, unusual trees & shrubs, perennials, annuals, natives, water elements, statuary, tree carvings.

Vanderburgh County
Indiana

Mesker Park Zoo & Botanical Garden

66

Mesker Park Drive

Mesker Park Zoo

Evansville

62

Ohio River

66

Mesker Park Zoo

Main Entrance
Mesker Park Drive

Bement Avenue

North St. Joseph Avenue

N

Australia

Asian Valley

Klev Building

Lake Victoria

Discovery Center

African Panorama

African Rift

Main Parking

Main Entrance

North Parking

Events Area

Mesker Park Dr.

Amazonia Conservatory

North America

Bement Avenue

41. MESKER PARK ZOO & BOTANICAL GARDEN
EVANSVILLE, INDIANA

Southern Indiana's oldest zoo is home to hundreds of domestic and exotic animals as well as hundreds of native and exotic botanical specimens. The gently rolling 45 lush acres are beautifully landscaped to complement the animal exhibits. The all-weather paths are lined with educational and ornamental garden plantings and the climate controlled interior of the Kiev Building, Discovery Center and Amazonia house specialty installations of plant life that are labeled for easy identification.

> *"A garden is a friend you can visit anytime."*
> **Anonymous**

More than 500 trees are tagged and identified, providing summer shade for visitors and for many of the 700 animals who are residents. Tropical and subtropical exotics are planted outside in protected areas during the warm months. Amazonia, the Forest of Riches, is a recent addition to the city-owned and maintained facility. The 50-foot-tall conservatory features a South American rain forest filled with the flora and fauna of the vast tropical region. Over 250 neo-tropical plant species including various trees, palms, *heliconias*, *anthuriums*, orchids, *bromeliads*, and *philodendrons* thrive under the conditions created by the rain and fog systems.

Mesker Park is virtually a "living museum" and a highly rewarding experience for visitors to observe a wide range of plants and animals from around the world. True to its mission statement, Mesker Park Zoo and Botanical Garden does "foster the preservation of Earth's diverse species" especially through educational programs and events that raise environmental awareness.

Additional attractions and amenities include group tours, facility rental, concessions, gift shops, preservation programs and membership.

*Mesker Park Zoo & Botanical Garden, 1545 Mesker Park Dr., Evansville, IN 47720 **Tel:** (812) 435-6143 **Web:** www.meskerparkzoo.com **Open:** daily, 9 a.m.-5 p.m. **Acreage:** 45 **Fee(s):** admission, facility rental, group tours, educational programs, special events, membership **Botanical Collections:** native & exotic annuals, perennials, shrubs, specimen trees, tropical conservatory.

Giraffe & Sycamore,
Mesker Park Zoo & Botanical Garden, Evansville

New Harmony Gardens

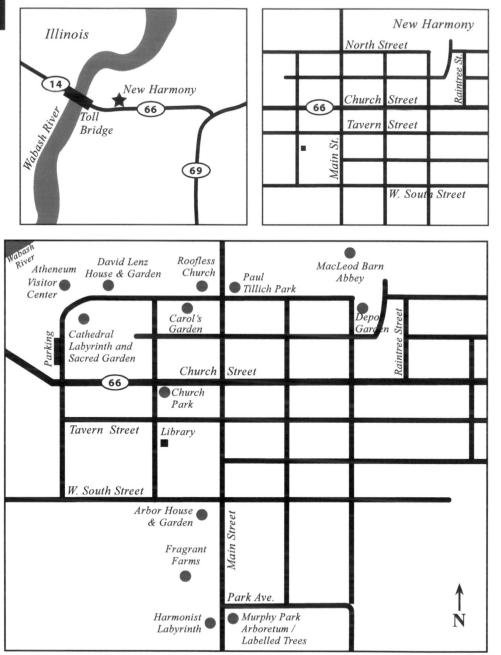

42. New Harmony Historic Sites & Gardens
New Harmony, Indiana

New Harmony, a National Historic Landmark, was the location of two experiments of communal-utopian-living experiments during the early 19th century. The first social experiment was founded by Father George Rapp and the Harmonie Society (1814-1824), a group of self-sufficient Separatists from the German Lutheran Church who immigrated to the United States and settled in Pennsylvania in 1804 from Wurttemberg, Germany. In 1825, when the Harmonists moved back to their spiritual sanctuary in Harmony, Pennsylvania, Robert Owen, Welsh-born industrialist, philanthropist, and social reformer purchased the town site for his communitarian experiment (1825-1827). Both communal groups relied on their own horticultural skills and practices to survive and flourish on the western edge of the new frontier.

Harmonist Garden, Lenz House, New Harmony

Today's visitor may discover New Harmony's rich horticultural past via the numerous tour sites and gardens that reveal the past and present social history of the community. The public-accessible gardens are owned and maintained by Historic New Harmony, the Indiana Department of Natural Resources, the Robert Lee Blaffer Foundation and many private citizens. Most of the gardens are located in a five-block east-to-west stretch along North Street on the north side of New Harmony, and they are self guiding, small in size and free to explore.

From the Atheneum/Visitors Center located at the corner of Arthur and North streets (where all tours begin), walking east along North Street to Raintree Street will lead visitors to the following historic and contemporary gardens: Cathedral Labyrinth and Sacred Garden, Harmonist David Lenz House and Garden, Carol's Garden, the Roofless Church, the Paul Tillich Park, and Our Lord's Wood. Several of the formal and informal gardens have water features such as fountains, along with statuary and benches are on hand to sit, contemplate and take in the aesthetic settings.

Church Park, located at the corner of Church and West streets, was built on the original site of the two Harmonist churches. It is a peaceful location in the center of town. A fountain sits in the middle of the formal gardens and the park is entered through a re-creation of the Door of Promise, which welcomed Harmonists to their large brick church.

Situated eight blocks south of the stoplight on Main Street/business S.R. 69 is the restored Harmonist Labyrinth. The labyrinth maze of privet hedge symbolizes the difficult journey to perfection and true harmony. The object of the maze is to discover the true path to heaven symbolized by the stone grotto at the center. In addition, nearby Fragrant Farms along W. South Street is a private farm that produces cut flowers, peonies and wine. Mid-to-late May is the best time to view the Signature Peony Collection. Murphy Park at South Main has several labeled trees scattered about the grounds.

> *"They will be surrounded by gardens, have abundance of space in all directions… They will have walks and plantations before them."*
> **Robert Owen**

*New Harmony Historic Sites & Gardens, Historic New Harmony, POB 579, New Harmony, IN 47631 **Tel:** (800) 231-2168 **Web:** www.newharmony.org **Open:** daily, gardens dawn to dusk **Acreage:** less than ten **Fee(s):** gardens none **Botanical Collections:** historic gardens, herbs, annuals, perennials, evergreens.

Quilt Garden, Ruthmere Mansion, Elkhart

Spring Flowering Bulbs, Oliver Winery, Bloomington

Significant Other Indiana Public Gardens

*Avon Perennial Gardens, 6259E CR 91N, Avon, IN 46123   **Tel:** (317) 272-6264
Web: www.avongardens.com   **Open:** Mon.-Tues.-, 10 a.m.-5 p.m., Wed.-Sat., 10 a.m.-7 p.m.   **Acreage:** 5
Fee(s): facility rental, special events   **Botanical Collections:** display gardens, water features.

*Barker Mansion & Civic Center Garden, 631 Washington St. at 7th St., Michigan City, IN 46360
Tel: (219) 873-1520   **Web:** www.emichigancity.com/barkermansion   **Open:** daily, June 1-Oct. 31, 10
a.m.-3 p.m., Nov. 1-May 31, Mon.-Fri., 10 a.m.-3 p.m., closed legal holidays   **Acreage:** less than one   **Fee(s):**
admission, facility rental, special events   **Botanical Collections:** Italianate sunken garden, English rose
garden, perennials, statuary, teahouse, pergola, courtyard.

*Battell Park, Mishawaka Parks & Recreation, 301 W. Mishawaka Ave., Mishawaka, IN 46544   **Tel:** (574)
258-1664   **Web:** www.mishawakacity.com/battellpark   **Open:** daily, sunrise to sunset   **Acreage:** garden
less than 3, 11 park total   **Fee(s):** facility rental   **Botanical Collections:** historic WPA-built terraced rock
garden, water features.

*Beutter Riverfront Park, Mishawaka Parks & Recreation, 400 N. Spring St., (sw corner of N. Main St.
bridge over St. Joseph River), Mishawaka, IN 46544   **Tel:** (574) 258-1664   **Web:** www.mishawakacity.
com/beautterpark   **Open:** daily, sunrise to sunset **Acreage:** 7   **Fee(s):** none   **Botanical Collections:**
perennial garden, sculpture, water elements.

*Blue River Nursery, 4484 E. Hartman Rd., Columbia City, IN 46725   **Tel:** (260) 244-7420   **Web:** www.
bluerivernursery.com   **Open:** March, 9 a.m.-6 p.m., closed July 4th   **Acreage:** 5 gardens, 40 total   **Fee(s):** none
Botanical Collections: display gardens.

*Bonneyville Mill County Park, 53373 CR 131, Bristol, IN 46507   **Tel:** (574) 535-6458   **Web:** www.
elkhartcountyparks.org   **Open:** seasonal hours   **Acreage:** gardens less than one, 222 park total   **Fee(s):** none
for garden, facility rental   **Botanical Collections:** herbs, dahlia test garden, perennials, annuals.

*Brinka-Cross Gardens, Porter County Parks & Recreation, 435 E. Furnessville Rd., Beverly Shores,
IN 46301   **Tel:** (219) 465-3586   **Web:** www.portercounty.org/parks   **Open:** May-Sept.   **Acreage:** 5
gardens, 26 total   **Fee(s):** facility rental   **Botanical Collections:** hostas, daylilies, Japanese tearoom, azaleas,
rhododendrons, evergreens, redwoods, magnolias, tallgrasses.

*Brookshire Arboretum, Lebanon Parks & Recreation, SR 39 (1.25 m. s. of Middle Jamestown Rd.), Lebanon, IN 46052 **Tel**: (765) 482-8860 **Web**: www.bccn.boone.in.us/lebanon/parks **Open**: daily, dawn to dusk **Acreage**: 14 **Fee(s)**: none **Botanical Collections**: native trees & shrubs.

*Carolee's Herb Farm & Garden, 3305 S. CR 100W, Harford City, IN 47348 **Tel**: (765) 348-3162 **Web**: www.caroleesherbfarm.com **Open**: April 1-Sept. 30, Tues.-Sat., 10 a.m.-5 p.m., closed Easter, Memorial Day, July 4, Labor Day **Acreage**: 11 **Fee(s)**: workshops, special events **Botanical Collections**: 20 display gardens, herbs, old fashioned flowers.

*Cherokee Ridge Gardens, 1101E Rt. #3, Solsberry, IN 47459 **Tel**: (812) 876-1349 **Web**: www. hometown.com/cherokeeridge **Open**: by appt. or 1 p.m.-6 p.m., Fri.-Sat., May-Oct. **Acreage**: 70 total **Fee(s)**: facility rental, special events **Botanical Collections**: display gardens, herbs, water gardens.

*Coburg Planting Fields, 573E CR 600N & CR 500E, Valparaiso, IN 46383 **Tel**: (219) 462-4288 **Web**: www.daylilytrader.com **Open**: for seasonal hours, email phil.brockington@valpo.edu **Acreage**: 10 **Fee(s)**: none **Botanical Collections**: American Hemerocallis Society display garden.

*Connor Prairie Living History Museum, 13400 Allisonville Rd., Fishers, IN 46038 **Tel**: (317) 776-6000, (800) 966-1836 **Web**: www.connorprairie.org **Open**: seasonal hours, closed Mondays & major holidays, April-Sept., Tues.-Sat., 10 a.m.-5 p.m., Sun. 11 a.m.-5 p.m. **Acreage**: 800 total **Fee(s)**: admission **Botanical Collections**: heirloom, homestead gardens, orchards.

*Crown Hill Cemetery, 700 W. 38th St., Indianapolis, IN 46208 **Tel**: (317) 925-8231, (800) 809-3366 **Web**: www.crownhill.org **Open**: daily, Oct.-March, 8 a.m.-5 p.m., April-Sept., 8 a.m.-6 p.m. **Acreage**: 555 **Fee(s)**: none **Botanical Collections**: arboretum.

*D'Vine Gallery Garden & Gift, 310 N. Harrison at Depot St., Shipshewana, IN 46565 **Tel**: (219) 768-7110, (800)-831-0504 **Web**: www.divinegallerygardenandgift.com **Open**: summer hours, Mon.-Sat., 10 a.m.-5 p.m.; winter hours, Tues.-Fri., 10 a.m.-5 p.m., Sat., 10 a.m.-3 p.m., closed Sundays **Acreage**: less than one **Fee(s)**: none **Botanical Collections**: display garden, herbs, lavender, Faerie Garden, statuary, greenhouse.

*Elkhart County Quilt Garden Tour, Amish Country Visitor Information, 219 Caravan Dr., Elkhart, IN 46514 **Tel:** (800) 377-3579 or 4827 **Web:** www.amishcountry.org **Open:** Memorial Day to frost **Acreage:** 12 separate Elkhart County gardens total 3 acres **Fee(s):** none **Botanical Collections:** 12 county-wide quilt-designed gardens feature 60,000 annuals.

*Dr. James Ford 1838 Historic Home, 177 W. Hill St., Wabash, IN 46992 **Tel:** (260) 563-8686 **Web:** www.jamesfordmuseum.org **Open:** Sat. 10 a.m.-5 p.m., Sun. 12 p.m.-5 p.m., also by appt. **Acreage:** less than one **Fee(s)** none for garden, facility rental, tour **Botanical Collections:** kitchen garden, medicinal herbs, Victorian-era flowers.

*Fort Wayne Parks & Recreation, 705 E. State Blvd., Ft. Wayne, IN 46805 **Tel:** (260) 427-6000 **Web:** www.fortwayneparks.org **Open:** daily, dawn to dusk: Jaenicke Park Garden at Greenwood Ave. in W. Swinney Park; Lawton Park Garden, 1900 Clinton & 4th St.; Swinney Homestead Herb Garden, E. Swinney Park, 1600 W. Jefferson Blvd. **Acreage:** less than 5 acres of gardens **Fee(s):** none **Botanical Collections:** annuals, perennials, herbs.

*Fulton County Public Library Arboretum, 320 W. 7th St., Rochester, IN 46975 **Tel:** (574) 223-2713 **Web:** www.fulco.lib.in.us/arboretum **Open:** daily, dawn to dusk **Acreage:** 2 **Fee(s):** none **Botanical Collections:** native & exotic trees & shrubs.

*Heritage Gardens at St. Patricks County Park, 50651 Laurel Rd., South Bend, IN 46637 **Tel:** (574) 277-4828 **Web:** www.sjcparks.org/stpats **Open:** daily, seasonal hours vary, closed major holidays **Acreage:** 30 acres of gardens, 398 total **Fee(s):** admission, facility rental **Botanical Collections:** Adair orchard, grapes, small fruit.

*Hidden Hill Nursery & Sculpture Garden, 1011 Utica-Charlestown Rd., Utica, IN 47130 **Tel:** (812) 282-0524 **Web:** www.hiddenhillnursery.com **Open:** Fri., 10 a.m.-7 p.m., Sat., 9 a.m.-7 p.m., Sun. noon-5 p.m., or by appt. **Acreage:** 5 **Fee(s);** none **Botanical Collections:** arboretum, sculpture.

*Hobbit Gardens, 6213 E. CR 300N, (3 miles n. of Fillmore) Fillmore, IN 46128 **Tel:** (765) 246-6315 **Web:** www.hobbitgardens.hendrickscountyconnection.com **Open:** year around, Tues., 10 a.m.-5 p.m., Thurs.-Fri., 10 a.m.-7 p.m., Sat., 10 a.m.-5 p.m., Sun., 1 p.m.-5 p.m. **Acreage:** 27.5 **Fee(s):** none for gardens, workshops, plant sales, special events, gift shop **Botanical Collections:** herbs, flowers, display gardens.

*Holliday Park, Indy Metro Parks, 6363 Spring Mill Rd., Indianapolis, IN 46260 **Tel**: (317) 327-7180 **Web**: www.hollidaypark.org **Open**: daily, sunrise to sunset **Acreage**: 94 **Fee(s)**: none **Botanical Collections**: arboretum, rock garden, native wildflowers, prairie.

*Hoosier Heritage Garden, Governor's Residence, 4750 N. Meridian St. (46th & Meridian), Indianapolis, IN 46208 **Tel**: (317) 931-3076 or 831-7980 **Web**: www.in.gov/gov **Open**: pre-arranged group tours via mail **Acreage**: 6.5 **Fee(s)**: none **Botanical Collections**: formal garden, sculpture, peace garden, sunset terrace.

*Hoosier Woodland Arboretum Trail, Martin State Forest, POB 599, U.S. 50, Shoals, IN 47581 **Tel**: (812) 247-3491 **Web**: www.statepark.com/martin **Open**: daily, dawn to dusk **Acreage**: 3, 0.25 mile trail, 7,023 total **Fee(s)**: none **Botanical Collections**: arboretum, native trees, shrubs.

*Indiana Medical Museum, 3045 W. Vermont, Indianapolis, IN 46222 **Tel**: (317) 635-7329 **Web**: www.imhm.org **Open**: Thurs.-Sat., 10 a.m.- 4 p.m., also by appt. **Acreage**: less than one **Fee(s)**: admission **Botanical Collections**: medicinal herbs.

*Indiana State Museum, Watanabe Family Gardens, 650 W. Washington St., Indianapolis, IN 46206 **Tel**: (317) 232-1637 **Web**: www.in.gov./ism/watgardens **Open**: daily, dawn to dusk **Acreage**: less than 2 **Fee(s)**: none for gardens **Botanical Collections**: native flowers, grasses.

*Kate's Garden, Mishawaka Parks & Recreation, 1202 Lincolnway W., Mishawaka, IN 46544 **Tel**: (574) 258-1664 **Web**: www.mishawakacity.com/parksandrecreation **Open**: daily, sunrise to sunset **Acreage**: 1.5 **Fee(s)**: facility rental **Botanical Collections**: annuals, perennials, shrubs, sculpture.

*Moraine Arboretum, Lemon Lake County Park, 6322 W. 133 Ave. Crown Point, IN 46307 **Tel**: (219) 945-0543 **Web**: www.lakecountyparks.org **Open**: daily, 7 a.m.-sunset **Acreage**: 5 arboretum, 403 park total **Fee(s)**: park admission **Botanical Collections**: arboretum.

*Oliver Winery Gardens, 8024 N. SR 37, Bloomington, IN 47404 **Tel**: (812) 876-5800 **Web**: www.oliverwinery.com **Open**: daily, Mon.-Sat., 10 a.m.-6 p.m., Sun., noon-6 p.m., closed major holidays & election day **Acreage**: 15 **Fee(s)**: none **Botanical Collections**: annuals, perennials, shrubs, native wildflowers, sculpture, water elements.

*One-Hundred Trees of Indiana Walking Trail, Indiana State University, Brown & Wabash Aves. (U.S. 40 & ISU Memorial Stadium), Terre Haute, IN 47801 **Tel**: (812) 462-3371 **Web**: www.treesinc. org/indiana **Open**: daily, daylight hours **Acreage**: one mile trail encircling ISU stadium **Fee(s)**: none **Botanical Collections**: native tree arboretum.

*Pioneer Interpretive Garden, Brown County State Park, 1405 SR 46, Nashville, IN 47448 **Tel**: (812) 988-6406 **Web**: www.in.gov/dnr/parklake **Open**: daily, sunrise to sunset **Acreage**: less than one **Fee(s)**: park admission **Botanical Collections**: pioneer garden, herbs, annuals, perennials.

*Quail Ridge Farm Nursery & Landscape, 3382 E. 1000N, Hesston, IN 46350 **Tel**: (219) 778-2194 or (800) 757-7752 **Web**: www.park.org **Open**: 9 a.m.-5 p.m., daily, May 1 to Oct. 31 **Acreage**: 20 **Fee(s)**: none **Botanical Collections**: Shakespeare Garden, rose, Japanese, alpine rock, woodland, pond, prairie, Native American.

*James Whitcomb Riley Boyhood Home & Museum, 250 W. Main, Greenfield, IN 46140 **Tel**: (317) 477-4340 or 462-8539 **Web**: www.greenfieldin.org **Open**: April 5-Nov. 6, Mon.-Sat., 10 a.m.-4 p.m., Sun., 1 p.m.-4 p.m. **Acreage**: less than one **Fee(s)**: tours **Botanical Collections**: old fashioned herbs, thyme collection, flowers.

*Ruthmere, 302 E. Beardsley Ave., Elkhart, IN 46514 **Tel**: (574) 264-0330 or (888) 287-7696 **Web**: www.ruthmere.org **Open**: April 1 to Dec. 14, Tues.-Fri., 11 a.m.-3 p.m., Wed. until 7 p.m. **Acreage**: garden less than one acre **Fee(s)**: admission tours, facility rental **Botanical Collections**: Italian formal garden, annual perennials, Elkhart County quilt garden.

*Willowfield Lavender Farm, 6176 E. Smokey View Rd., Mooresville, IN 46158 **Tel**: (317) 831-7980 **Web**: www.willowfieldlavender.com **Open**: May-Sept., Thurs, Fri. & Sat., 10 a.m.-4 p.m. **Acreage**: 28 **Fee(s)**: none**Botanical Collections**: commercial lavender farm.

*Witmer Woods Arboretum, Goshen College, Reservoir Place Dr., Goshen, IN 46526 **Tel**: (800) 348-7422 **Web**: www.goshen.edu **Open**: daily, dawn to dusk **Acreage**: 18 **Fee(s)**: none **Botanical Collections**: native arboretum.

Heritage Garden, Chicago Botanic Garden, Glencoe, Illinois

Baha'i House of Worship Gardens, Wilmette, Illinois

GREATER CHICAGO PUBLIC GARDENS

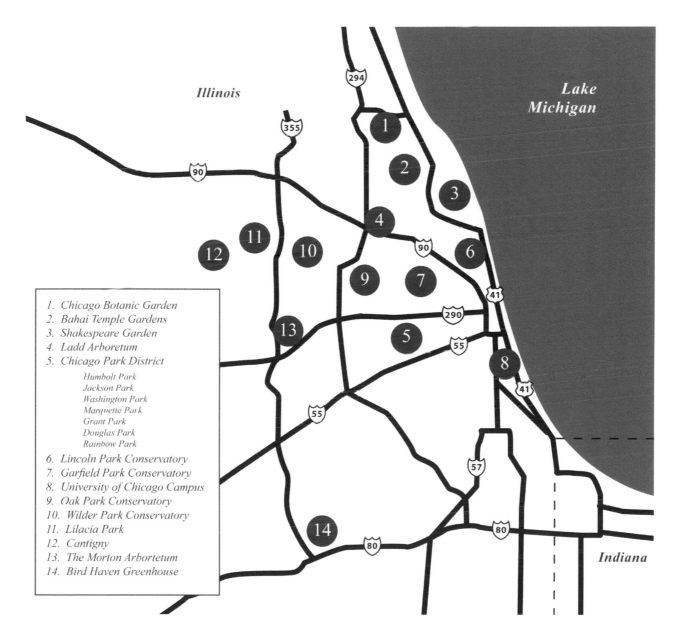

Illinois

Lake
Michigan

1. Chicago Botanic Garden
2. Bahai Temple Gardens
3. Shakespeare Garden
4. Ladd Arboretum
5. Chicago Park District

    Humbolt Park
    Jackson Park
    Washington Park
    Marquette Park
    Grant Park
    Douglas Park
    Rainbow Park

6. Lincoln Park Conservatory
7. Garfield Park Conservatory
8. University of Chicago Campus
9. Oak Park Conservatory
10. Wilder Park Conservatory
11. Lilacia Park
12. Cantigny
13. The Morton Arbortetum
14. Bird Haven Greenhouse

Indiana

1. Chicago Botanic Garden
Glencoe, Illinois

Operated by the Chicago Horticultural Society, the Chicago Botanic Garden officially opened in 1972 and is now one of America's premier public gardens. The 385 acreage is divided into areas of garden displays (60 acres), native habitats, lagoons, lakes, islands and facilities. There are 23 specialty gardens and three natural areas situated on and around nine lakes. The botanic garden offers educational programs, special events, facility rentals, horticultural information and a library.

*Chicago Botanic Garden, 1000 Lake Cook Rd. (20 miles north of Chicago), P. O. Box 400, Glencoe, IL 60022 Tel: (847)-835-5440 Web: www.chicago-botanic.org Open: daily, 8 a.m.-7 p.m., closed Christmas Acreage: 385 Fee(s): admission parking, programs, facility rental, special events, tram tours, garden membership, donations accepted Botanical Collections: arboretum, conservatory, aquatic garden, cottage garden, Japanese garden, herbs, rose, sensory, enabling garden, xeriscape, native plants, statuary, carillon.

2. Baha'i House of Worship Gardens
Wilmette, Illinois

Established in 1953, the landmark Baha'i House of Worship is surrounded by a series of gardens and fountains. The nine separate gardens are arranged in a pie-shaped circle, unified around the central, lotus flower-shaped House of Worship that required eight years to construct. The beautiful site is listed in the National Register of Historic Places.

*Baha'i House of Worship Gardens, 100 Linden Ave. at Sheridan Rd., Wilmette, IL 60091 Tel: (847) 853-2396 Web: www.us.bahai.org Open: daily, garden dawn to dusk; visitor center, May thru Sept., 10 a.m.-8p.m., Oct.-April, 10 a.m.-5 p.m. Acreage: less than ten Fee(s): donations accepted Botanical Collections: bulbs, perennials, annuals, shrubs, trees, water features.

3. Shakespeare Garden at Northwestern University
Evanston, Illinois

Listed on the National Register of Historic Place, the Shakespeare Garden was designed by prairie landscape architect, Jens Jensen in 1915, and installed during the 1920s. The garden was dedicated in 1930 in celebration of the ties between England and the United States, 300 years since the death of William Shakespeare. Maintained by the Evanston Garden Club, the Tudor-era English garden includes eight flower-filled beds containing such herbs and flowers as rosemary, lavender, thyme, hyssop, columbine, daffodil, poppy and marigolds, plants mentioned in Shakespeare's plays and sonnets. The gardens are situated between the Dearborn Observatory and Garrett Seminary at the campus of Northwestern University.

*Shakespeare Garden at Northwestern University, 1967 Sheridan Rd. & Garrett Rd. (12 miles north of Chicago), Evanston, IL 60201 **Tel**: (708) 491-4000, (312) 864-0655 **Web**: www. thegardencluboffevanston.org/gardens **Open**: daily, sunrise to sunset **Acreage**: 7,000 sq. ft. **Fee(s)**: none except for guided tours, facility rental **Botanical Collections**: Tudor-era English garden, perennials, annuals, shrubs, trees.

4. Ladd Arboretum
Evanston, Illinois

Occupying a narrow 0.75 mile stretch between McCormick Boulevard and the North Shore Channel, the Ladd Arboretum is named in honor of Edward Rixon Ladd, the founder, publisher and editor of the *Evanston Review*. Officially dedicated June 10, 1960, the arboretum's collection is arranged by plant family. Specialty garden collections include the Cherry Tree Walk, Nut Tree area, Meadow Garden, Prairie Restoration area, Rotary Friendship Garden, and Woman's Terrace. The Evanston Ecology Center is located on the southwest corner of Bridge Street and McCormick Boulevard. In addition, another Evanston city park garden to visit from June through October is the 0.5 acre Merrick Park Rose garden located at Lake and Oak streets.

*Ladd Arboretum, 2024 McCormick Blvd., Evanston, IL 60201 **Tel**: (847) 448-8256, (312) 864-5181 or 866-2910 **Web**: www.laddarboretum.org **Open**: daily, sunrise to sunset **Acreage**: 23 **Fee(s)**: programs, classes **Botanical Collections**: arboretum, cherry, nut trees, prairie, roses.

5. Chicago Park District
Chicago, Illinois

Several botanic sites in Chicago are located in the city parks. Noted landscape architects, Jens Jensen and Frederick Law Olmsted helped to design over 500 Chicago parks in the late 19th and early 20th centuries:

Humboldt Park - flower & sunken gardens, Division St. & Sacramento Blvd.
Jackson Park - Japanese Osaka Garden, 6401 S. Stony Island Ave. and the Perennial Sunken Garden, 59th & Stony Island Ave.

Douglas Park - formal garden, Ogden Ave. & Sacramento Blvd.

Grant Park - formal, annual, rose gardens, Court of President's Garden,
Michigan Ave. east to Lake Michigan.

Marquette Park - rose and trial garden, perennial, annual, shade, topiary,
6734 S. Kedzie Ave., 3540 W. 71ˢᵗ St.

Washington Park - arboretum, annual gardens, formal gardens,
E. 55ᵗʰ St. & Cottage Grove Ave., E. 51ˢᵗ, Elworth Dr., S. M. L. King Dr.

Rainbow Park - flower garden, 77ᵗʰ St. & 78th St., east of S. Shore Dr.

*__Chicago Park District__, Dept. of Public Information, 425 E. McFetridge Dr., Chicago, IL 60605 **Tel:** (312) 747-2474 or 294-2493 **Web:** www.chicagoparkdistrict.com **Open:** daily, grounds, gardens, 7 a.m.-11 p.m. **Acreage:** 7,000 acres total **Fee(s):** none for gardens, facility rental **Botanical Collections:** arboretum, annuals, perennials, formal, sunken, Japanese, trial, rose gardens, conservatories at Lincoln & Garfield parks.

6. Lincoln Park Conservatory
Chicago, Illinois

Erected in 1891 and designed by architect Joseph L. Silsbee, the three-acre Lincoln Park Conservatory showcases houses of cactus, ferns, palms and orchids along with other tropical flora plus special seasonal flower shows and events. Outside, the seven-acre Lincoln Park Great Garden includes a color-filled mix of display gardens, lawns, fountains and statuary. The first garden to be established in the Chicago Park District is the 1893 Grandmother's Garden that is situated outside the Lincoln Park Zoo near Stockton Drive and Webster Avenue.

*__Lincoln Park Conservatory,__ 2400 N. Stockton Dr., Chicago, IL 60614 Tel: (312) 742-7736 **Web:** www.chicagoparkdistrict.com **Open:** daily, 9 a.m.-5 p.m. **Acreage:** conservatory 3, gardens 7 **Fee(s):** guided tours, lectures, special events, donations accepted **Botanical Collections:** conservatory, tropicals, subtropicals, formal gardens, shade & flowering trees, conifer garden, Grandmother's Garden.

7. Garfield Park Conservatory
Chicago, Illinois

Designed by Jens Jensen, Prairie School landscape architect and West Parks Superintendent, the Garfield Park Conservatory was considered "landscape art under glass" and the "largest public conservatory worldwide" when it first opened in 1908. Today, the 4.5 acre conservatory is considered one of Chicago's premier botanical institutions. The conservatory includes the Palm Room (84 varieties),

Aroid Tropical House, a Fernery (100 species), Cactus House, Children's Garden, Economic Plant House and Horticultural Hall. Renovated in 1994, there is also a library and classes are programs are held year-around. Outside the four acres of gardens include 24 flower beds, water lily lagoons and an Urban Demonstration Garden. The Garfield Park Conservatory is listed on the National Register of Historic Places.

*Garfield Park Conservatory, 300 N. Central Park Ave., Chicago, IL 60624 **Tel:** (773) 746-5100 **Web:** www.garfieldconservatory.org **Open:** daily, 9 a.m.-5 p.m., Thurs. until 8 p.m. **Acreage:** conservatory 4.5, park total 184 **Fee(s):** none for admittance, donations accepted, facility rental **Botanical Collections:** conservatory, tropicals, subtropicals, ferns, aroids, palms, cacti, flower display beds, fountains, lagoons.

8. University of Chicago Botanic Garden
Chicago, Illinois

The 211 acre campus of the University of Chicago features 24 campus gardens that include the Cloister Garden, Circle Garden, Butterfly Garden, Botany Pond, Nuclear Energy Garden and the World's Columbian Exposition Oak. The mission of the campus is to "grow, display and document plant materials suited to the environment of the Chicago lakefront." The elegant campus landscape is an official American Association of Botanical Gardens and Arborea site. A brochure is available.

*University of Chicago Botanic Garden, 5801 S. Ellis Ave., Rm. 7, Chicago, Il 60637 **Tel:** (773) 834-1657 **Web:** www.uchicago.edu **Open:** daily, daylight hours **Acreage:** 211 **Fee(s):** none **Botanical Collections:** arboretum, display gardens, perennials, annuals.

9. Oak Park Conservatory
Oak Park, Illinois

Built in 1929, the 8,000-square foot-conservatory features desert, tropical rainforest, ferns and subtropical plants. The Edwardian-styled glasshouse is the third largest conservatory in the Chicago area and contains more than 3,000 plants. Additional facilities include classrooms, herb and native prairie garden, a library and a new Urban Horticulture Education and Resource Center.

*Oak Park Conservatory, 615 Garfield St. at East Ave., Oak Park, IL 60304
Tel: (704) 386-4700 **Web:** www.oakparkparks.com/parks **Open:** daily, Tues.-Sunday, 10 a.m.-4 p.m., Monday, 2 p.m.-4 p.m., holidays, 10 a.m.-3 p.m. **Acreage:** 8,000 sq. ft. conservatory, 1 acre gardens **Fee(s):** donations accepted **Botanical Collections:** conservatory, desert, orchids, ferns, rainforest.

10. Wilder Park Conservatory
Elmhurst, Illinois

Owned and maintained by the Elmhurst Park District, Wilder Park Conservatory, greenhouse, gardens and park have a long horticultural history beginning in 1868. The city of Elmhurst acquired the private garden in the 1920s and built the conservatory in 1923.

Wilder Park Conservatory, 225 Prospect Ave., Elmhurst, Il 60126 **Tel:** (630) 993-8900 **Web:** www.epd.org **Open:** daily, 8 a.m.-4 p.m. **Acreage:** 13 acre park total **Fee(s):** facility rental, donations accepted **Botanical Collections:** conservatory, formal gardens.

11. Lilacia Park
Lombard, Illinois

This former private garden of Mr. and Mrs. Wm. R. Plum is now a city-owned horticultural park (est. 1927) and features 275 varieties of lilac shrubs (1,200 total) that flower from early to mid-May along with spring flowering bulbs. The garden was designed by noted landscape architect Jens Jensen. Several festivals and special events are held annually in Lilacia Park.

Lilacia Park, Parkside & Park Avenues, Lombard, IL 60148 **Tel:** (312) 627-1281 **Web:** www.lombardparks.com **Open:** daily, conservatory 9 a.m.-9 p.m. **Acreage:** 8.5 acre park total **Fee(s):** special events, programs, gift shop, facility rental **Botanical Collections:** lilacs, tulips, spring bulbs, flowering trees.

12. Cantigny
Wheaton, Illinois

Cantigny, the former estate of Chicago Tribune publisher, Col. Robert McCormick, is comprised of 25 acres of formal and informal gardens, hiking paths, picnic groves and two museums that are open to guided tours: the Robert B. McCormick Museum and the First Division Museum. The 20 thematic gardens are designed by landscape architect, Franz Lipp, and consist of the extensive use of annuals, perennials, ground covers, bulbs and wide variety of flowering and shade trees and shrubs. The gardens are interconnected by 2.5 miles of red brick paths and lawn. Garden themes include the Burr Oak, Fountain, Green, Scalloped, Children and Rose gardens and renovated prairie. Cantigny is named for the first American victory in WWI at the Battle of Cantigny, France, where Col. Robert R. McCormick served.

*Cantigny, 1 S. 151 Winfield Rd., (30 miles west of Chicago), Wheaton, IL 60187 **Tel:** (630) 668-5161 **Web:** www.cantigny.org **Open:** grounds, Tues.-Sunday, 9 a.m.-dusk, March-Dec. 31, closed January, Fri.-Sun., 9 a.m. - dusk in February **Acreage:** gardens 10, total 500 **Fee(s):** admission parking, guide group tours, museums, special events, programs, musical events **Botanical Collections:** estate garden, spring bulbs, annuals, topiary, formal gardens, arboretum, demonstration gardens, thematic gardens, prairie-savannah.

13. The Morton Arboretum
Lisle, Illinois

Established in 1922, the Morton Arboretum began on the estate grounds of Mr. Joy Morton, son of W. Sterling Morton, the founder of Arbor Day in 1872. The botanic collection includes 40,000 plants, 4,000 types of plants worldwide. Bisected by Illinois SR 53, the arboretum's natural areas are accessible by eight miles of road and 16 miles of foot trails. Thematic gardens include the Hedge Garden, Rose garden, Children's Garden, Fragrance Garden and Ground Cover Garden. Additional amenities include a library, herbarium, picnic area, gift shop, tram, café, restaurant, plant clinic, educational center, programs, publications and plant sales.

*The Morton Arboretum, 4100 Illinois SR 53, (north of I-88, 25 miles west of Chicago), Lisle, IL 60532 **Tel:** (630) 968-0074 or 719-2400 **Web:** www.mortonarb.org **Open:** daily, CDT 7 a.m.-7 p.m., CST 7 a.m.-5 p.m. or sunset **Acreage:** 1,700 total **Fee(s):** admission parking, facility rental, special events, garden membership, programs **Botanical Collections:** arboretum, special woody plant collections, tall grass prairie, thematic gardens.

14. Bird Haven Conservatory & Greenhouse
Joliet, Illinois

Built in the early 1900s, the Italian Renaissance-styled conservatory was designed by the noted firm of Lord & Burnham. A tropical room, cacti and succulent room, seasonal floral show room and recently added children's garden comprise the conservatory which is accessible via cobblestone and paved walkways. The outdoor gardens are filled with annuals and perennial flowering plants that add to the gracious setting. A Joliet Park District facility, Bird Haven is located in Pilcher Park at the east edge of the city.

*Bird Haven Conservatory & Greenhouse, Pilcher Park, 225 N. Gougar Rd., Joliet, IL 60432 **Tel**: (815) 741-7278 **Web**:www.jolietpark.org **Open**: daily, 8 a.m.-4:30 p.m., including holidays **Acreage**: 3 grounds, greenhouse & gardens, 660 park total **Fee(s)**: donations accepted, facility rental **Botanical Collections**: conservatory, tropical, subtropical, annuals, perennials, seasonal floral shows.

Cantigny, Wheaton, Illinois

Shakespeare Garden, Northwestern University, Evanston, Illinois

Garfield Park Conservatory, Chicago, Illinois

Flowering Rhododendron, Aullwood Gardens, Dayton, Ohio

Dragonfly Pond, Children's Discovery Garden, Wergerzyn Gardens, Dayton, Ohio

GREATER DAYTON PUBLIC GARDENS

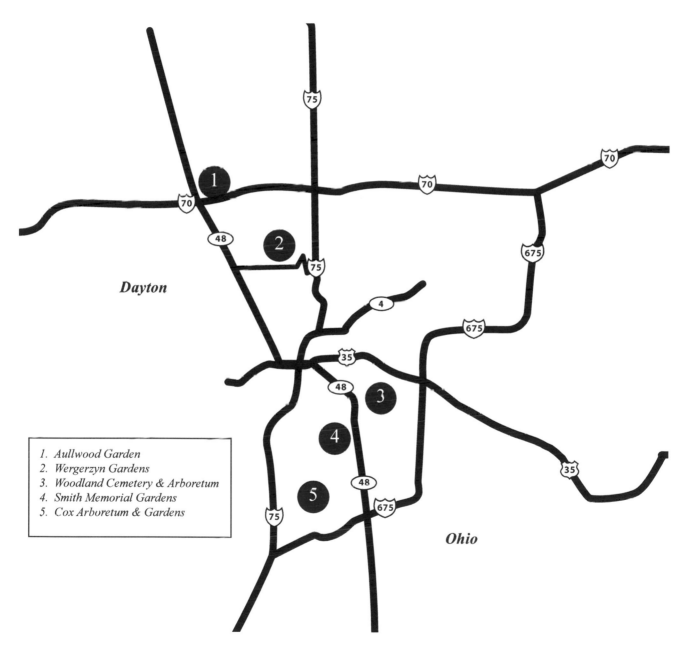

1. Aullwood Garden
2. Wergerzyn Gardens
3. Woodland Cemetery & Arboretum
4. Smith Memorial Gardens
5. Cox Arboretum & Gardens

1. Aullwood Garden
Dayton, Ohio

Naturalized woodland gardens and meadow-lawn gardens surround the former home of conservationists, John and Marie Aull who moved here in 1923. Paths lead alongside Wiles Creek where wildflower-filled woodlands thrive. Virginia bluebells, blue-eyed Mary, celandine wood poppy, hepaticas, trilliums, shooting star and violet are common. In the meadow-lawn gardens, daffodils, hyacinth, primrose, rose, lilac and rhododendrons are cultivated. A ten-acre prairie is being restored. The property is listed on the National Historic Registry and is managed as a Five River Metro Park.

*Aullwood Garden, 900 Aullwood Rd., Dayton, OH 45414 **Tel:** (937) 275-PARK **Web:** www. metroparks.org **Open:** April 1-Oct. 31, 8 a.m.-10 p.m., Nov. 1-March 31, 8 a.m.-8 p.m., closed Christmas & New Year's Day **Acreage:** 32 total **Fee(s):** none for gardens, facility rental, garden membership **Botanical Collections:** wildflowers, prairies, rock garden, rose garden, peonies, lilacs, perennials, trees, shrubs.

2. Wergerzyn Gardens
Dayton, Ohio

This garden complex includes formal gardens, a Children's Discovery Garden and a 350-foot long swamp forest boardwalk. The formal gardens feature Federal, English and Victorian landscape styles. There are fountains, arbors, vases, parterres and plazas surrounding the garden green allee. The Children's Discovery Garden has habitat areas and several theme gardens. The swamp forest boardwalk is hooked into the one-mile Marie Aull Nature Trail within the Stillwater River floodplain. Year-round educational programs are offered and are held in the Wergerzyn Center. Community gardens are popular.

*Wergerzyn Gardens, 1301 E. Siebenthaler Ave., Dayton, OH 45414 **Tel:** (937) 277-6545 **Web:** www.metroparks.org **Open:** April 1-Oct. 31, 8 a.m.-10 p.m.; Nov. 1-March 31, 8 a.m.-8 p.m., closed Christmas & New Year's Day **Fee(s):** facility rental, educational programs, special events **Botanical Collections:** formal gardens, annuals, perennials, Children's Garden, trees, shrubs, swamp forest.

3. Woodland Cemetery & Arboretum
Dayton, Ohio

Established in 1841, the 200-acre rolling hills of Woodland Cemetery contain over 3,000 trees, many over a century old. Richly diverse, there are over 165 native woody species including nine Ohio champion trees. Located south of downtown near the University of Dayton, the site occupies the highest elevation in the city.

*Woodland Cemetery, 118 Woodland Ave., Dayton, OH 45409 **Tel:** (937) 228-3221 **Web:** www.woodlandcemetery.org **Open:** daily, 8:30 a.m.-5 p.m. **Acreage:** 200 **Fee(s):** donations accepted **Botanical Collections:** arboretum.

4. Smith Memorial Gardens
Dayton, Ohio

A small suburban green oasis, Smith Memorial Gardens was landscaped in the 1930s by former owners and donors, Carlton and Jeanette Smith. The scenic public garden features a koi filled pond with surrounding perennial flowers, trees and shrubs. The botanic site is popular for picnicking, children's story hour and concert series. The garden is managed as an Oakwood city park and is maintained by the Friends of Smith Gardens.

*Smith Memorial Gardens, 800 block of Oakwood Ave. & Walnut Lane, Oakwood, OH 45419 **Tel:** (937) 296-0775 **Web:** www.mvcc.net/oakwood **Open:** daily, daylight hours **Acreage:** less than 2 **Fee(s):** donations accepted, facility rental **Botanical Collections:** perennials, woody plants, water garden.

5. Cox Arboretum & Gardens
Dayton, Ohio

Founded in 1962, the Cox Arboretum and Garden grounds was a gift in 1972 from the James M. Cox Jr. family. Today, the 189-acre Fiver Rivers Metropark cultivates a wide variety of plants for education and aesthetics. In addition to the hundreds of labeled woody plants, there are several specialty gardens: Water, Stonewall Perennial, Rock, Synoptic, Shrub, Rose, Edible Landscape, Herb, Woodland, Japanese, Meditation and Wildflower. Additional features and elements include a butterfly house and meadow, a crab apple allee, children's maze, Compost Kitchen and Conservation Corner. Specialty plant collections include a red cedar grove, conifer, hosta, ferns, magnolias, clematis arbor, and ornamental grasses. There are 3.5 miles of trails that meander through meadow and forest. The education center complex includes facilities such as a gallery, theatre, classrooms, gift shop and library.

*Cox Arboretum, 6733 Springboro Pike/SR 741, Dayton, OH 45449 **Tel:** (937) 434-9005 **Web:** www.metropark.org **Open:** grounds, daily, April 1- Oct.31, 8 a.m.-10 p.m.; Nov. 1-March 31, 8 a.m.-8 p.m. **Acreage:** 189 **Fee(s):** donations accepted, facility rental, educational programs, workshops, special events **Botanical Collections:** arboretum, specialty gardens.

Succulent House, Krohn Conservatory, Cincinnati, Ohio

Overlook, Mt. Airy Arboretum, Cincinnati, Ohio

GREATER CINCINNATI PUBLIC GARDENS

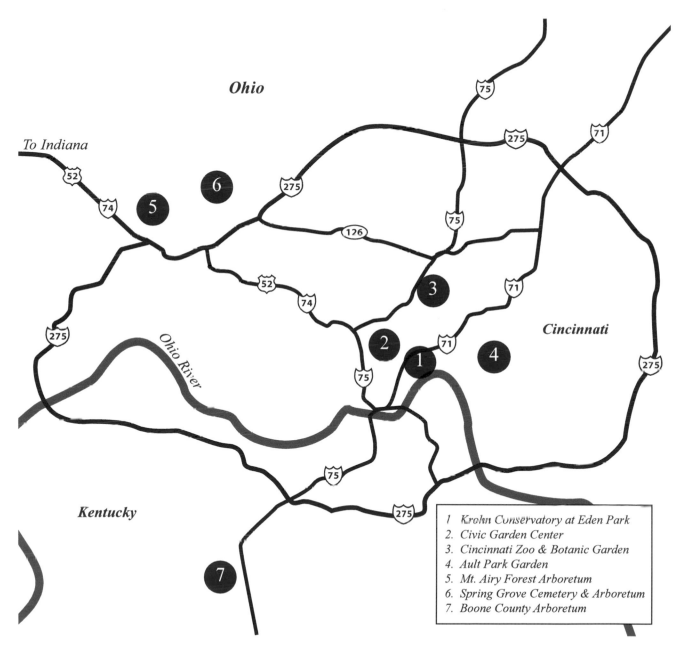

Ohio

To Indiana

Ohio River

Cincinnati

Kentucky

1   Krohn Conservatory at Eden Park
2. Civic Garden Center
3. Cincinnati Zoo & Botanic Garden
4. Ault Park Garden
5. Mt. Airy Forest Arboretum
6. Spring Grove Cemetery & Arboretum
7. Boone County Arboretum

1. **Krohn Conservatory at Eden Park**
   Cincinnati, Ohio

Completed in 1933, the Irwin M. Krohn Conservatory shelters four permanent display houses: palm, tropical, desert and orchid, and one seasonal floral display house. The 20,000-square-foot Gothic-Art Deco-styled structure shelters 3,500 plant species and a 20-foot rainforest waterfall. The seasonal display house features six floral shows a year. The Friends of Krohn Conservatory is an active support group. West of the conservatory is the Hinkle Garden with its magnolia collection. Additional botanic sites within Eden Park include the Liberty Memorial 9-11 Garden, the Presidential Grove and the 1904 Spring Gazebo House overlooking Mirror Lake and the Ohio River valley.

*Krohn Conservatory at Eden Park**, 1501 Eden Park Dr., Cincinnati, OH 45202 **Tel:** (513) 421-5707 or 352-3380 or 4080 **Web:** www.cincinnati-oh.gov/parks **Open:** daily, 10 a.m.–5 p.m., extended hours special shows & events **Acreage:** Krohn less than 5, 186 park total **Fee(s):** donations welcome, facility rental **Botanical Collections:** conservatory, tropical, desert.

2. **Civic Garden Center of Greater Cincinnati-Hauck Botanic Garden**
   Cincinnati, Ohio

Established in 1942, the environmental education center is an urban sanctuary in a former residential neighborhood, and has several specialized gardens that include collections of dahlia, daylily, hosta, daffodil, a shade garden, dwarf conifers, butterfly and herbs. Affectionately called "Sooty Acres", the arboretum portion of the botanic garden showcases over 900 varieties of woody plants. Special events, meetings, workshops, and horticultural lectures take place throughout the year. A horticultural library is open to the public and garden members.

*Civic Garden Center of Greater Cincinnati**, 2715 Reading Rd., Cincinnati, OH 45206 **Tel:** (513) 221-8733 **Web:** www.civicgardencenter.org **Open:** daily, grounds dawn to dusk **Acreage:** 8 total **Fee(s):** donations accepted, programs, special events, garden membership **Botanical Collections:** herbs, butterfly garden, rose, dahlia, shade, spring bulbs, special tree & flower collections.

3. **Cincinnati Zoo & Botanical Garden**
   Cincinnati, Ohio

Opened in 1875, the Cincinnati Zoo & Botanical Garden is the second oldest public zoological installation in the United States (after Philadelphia). The city-owned facility is noted for promoting conservation and research and for its endangered species and birthing programs. Attractive, educational and naturalistic floral settings are provided for the animal exhibits. There are 3,000 plant varieties that represent flora from around the world. The various gardens include the Pollinator Garden, Butterfly Garden, Dinosaur Garden, Oriental Garden, Garden of Peace, Endangered Species Garden, Native Plant Garden, The Rain Garden, plus several more.

*Cincinnati Zoo & Botanical Garden, 3400 Vine St., Cincinnati, OH 45220 Tel: (513) 961-1870 Web: www.cincinnatizoo.org/plants Open: daily, seasonal hours, May 24-Sept. 1st, 9 a.m.-6 p.m.; Sept. 2-Dec. 1st, 9 a.m.-5 p.m., closed Jan. 1-May 24, also Christmas and Thanksgiving Acreage: 75 Fee(s): admission, parking, facility rental, special events, educational programs, membership Botanical Collections: annuals, perennials, rare & endangered plants, woody plants.

4. Ault Park Gardens
Cincinnati, Ohio

Originally designed by George Kessler of the "Civic Beautification Movement," Ault Park is the fourth largest Cincinnati city park. Established in 1911, the formal display gardens are situated near the majestic Italian renaissance-styled pavilion, flanking both sides of the central allee mall and concert green. Flowering crab and cherry trees line the all-weather walkways and flowing fountains add beauty to the eloquent scene. Volunteer-supported adopt-a-plot gardens line the walks and include a Rock Garden, Japanese Garden, Culinary Herb Garden, Blue Flower Garden, plus more. A Rose Garden displays old fashioned roses. The "Trees for your Yard" arboretum displays shade and flowering trees. One of the nation's dahlia test plots is planted here. Spectacular skyline vistas of the Little Miami River valley from the upper pavilion and nearby overlook add further interest along with picnicking, playgrounds and trails.

*Ault Park Gardens, east end of 3600 Observatory Ave. in Hyde Park neighborhood, Cincinnati, OH 45208 Tel: (513) 956-9676 Web: www.aultparkac.org Open: daily, dawn to dusk Acreage: 224 total Fee(s): facility rental, special events Botanical Collections: formal gardens, thematic gardens, old fashioned roses, trees, dahlia, hardy succulents.

5. Mt. Airy Forest Arboretum
Cincinnati, Ohio

The first-purchased acreage for Mt. Airy Forest was in 1911 near the crest of Colerain Hill, thus began the first municipal reforestation project in the United States. Today, the hills and valleys of Mt. Airy Forest total 1,470 acres, the largest Cincinnati park facility. A prime feature of the park is the 120-acre arboretum which showcases more than 5,000 plants representing 1,600 species and varieties of woody plants. An outstanding conifer collection is located around the shores of the spring-fed Meyer Lake. There are also labeled collections of rhododendrons, azaleas, vines, herbs and shrubs. In addition, hiking trails, picnic shelters and tables, playgrounds and playfields are available in Mt. Airy Forest.

*Mt. Airy Forest Arboretum, 5083 Colerain Ave. (U.S. 27), Cincinnati, OH 45223 **Tel:** (513) 541-2510, 352-4060 **Web:** www.cincinnati-oh.gov/parks **Open:** daily, dawn to dusk **Acreage:** arboretum 120, total 1,469 **Fee(s):** facility rental **Botanical Collections:** arboretum, perennials, special collections.

6. Spring Grove Cemetery & Arboretum
Cincinnati, Ohio

Founded in 1845, Spring Grove Cemetery is home to 21 Ohio state champion trees and two national champions. Originating with a commitment to naturalistic landscape design, the cemetery arboretum has a rich horticulture tradition. In addition to the extensive collection of 800 types of native and exotic tree varieties, there are an abundant water element of 14 lakes, streams, waterfalls and fountains. Thousands of spring flowering bulbs, annuals, and perennials including a rose garden have been planted. Guidebooks may be obtained from the visitor center and guided tours are available.

*Spring Grove Cemetery & Arboretum, 4521 Spring Grove Ave., Cincinnati, OH 45232 **Tel:** (513) 853-7526 **Web:** www.springgrove.org **Open:** daily, 8 a.m.- 6 p.m. **Acreage:** 733 total **Fee(s):** none **Botanical Collections:** arboretum, ornamental flowers, rose garden.

7. Boone County Arboretum at Central Park
Union, Kentucky

Across the Ohio River from Cincinnati is the nation's first arboretum established within an active recreational park setting. Labeled woody plantings line the 2.2 mile long paved walking and exercise trail. Currently, there are over 1,100 trees and over 1,700 shrubs planted. The Boone County Cooperative

Extension Service and the supportive Friends of the Arboretum are working partners in promoting an appreciation and study of woody plants in the Tri-State region. In addition to the arboretum, the collections include native Kentucky grassland, ornamental grasses and bamboo and a children's garden. Special events and programs are held during the year.

*Boone County Arboretum at Central Park, 9190 Camp Ernst Rd., Union, KY 41091 **Tel:** (859) 384-4999 **Web:** www.bcarboretum.org **Open:** daily, dawn to dusk **Acreage:** 121 total **Fee(s):** facility rental, membership **Botanical Collections:** arboretum, prairie, ornamental grasses, children's garden, native woodland.

Knot Garden,
Civic Garden Center of Greater Cincinnati

Red Dogwood & Statuary, Cave Hill Cemetery, Louisville, Kentucky

Springtime at Historic Farmington, Louisville, Kentucky

GREATER LOUISVILLE PUBLIC GARDENS

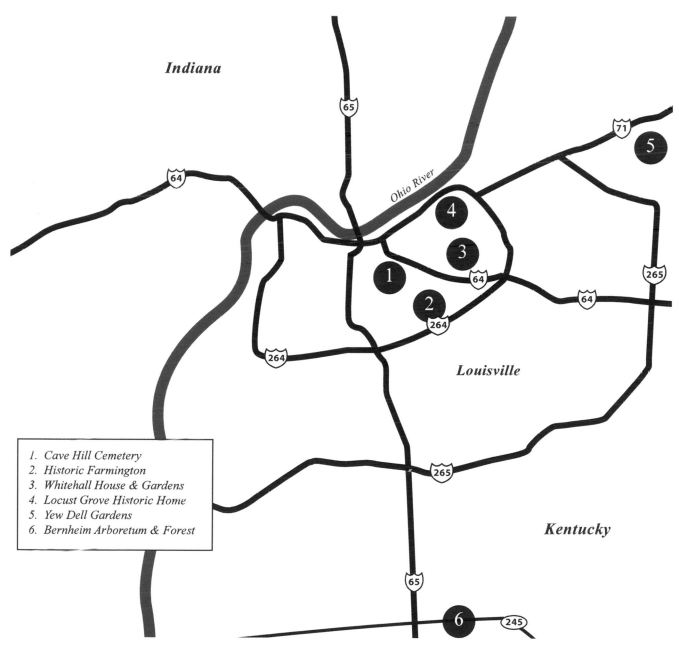

Indiana

Ohio River

Louisville

Kentucky

1. *Cave Hill Cemetery*
2. *Historic Farmington*
3. *Whitehall House & Gardens*
4. *Locust Grove Historic Home*
5. *Yew Dell Gardens*
6. *Bernheim Arboretum & Forest*

1. Cave Hill Cemetery
Louisville, Kentucky

Dedicated in 1848, Cave Hill Cemetery is Louisville's only arboretum. Once a farm, Cave Hill now harbors a wide diversity of trees and shrubs from around the world. Beautiful as well as historical, the 296 acres are landscaped in 19th century English pastoral tradition. There are 500 varieties of trees and shrubs. A tree brochure is available. Green tags identify 400 species of woody plants. Foot traffic is welcome along the 16 miles of paved roadways that interlace the memorial gardens. Points of interest include the restored Tingley Memorial Fountain, the Rustic Shelter House, the Tiffany Vase, five spring-fed lakes and one quarry.

*Cave Hill Cemetery, 701 Baxter Ave. (adjacent to Broadway, Cherokee Rd, Grinstead Dr. & Lexington Rd.), Louisville, KY 40204 **Tel:** (502) 451-5630 **Web:** www.cavehillcemetery.com **Open:** daily, 8 a.m.-4:45 p.m., weather permitting **Acreage:** 296 total **Fee(s):** facility rental **Botanical Collections:** arboretum, statuary, water elements.

2. Historic Farmington
Louisville, Kentucky

Historic Farmington is a restored Kentucky plantation home that was designed by Thomas Jefferson and built by John and Lucy Speed in 1816. The garden has been recreated with historical accuracy and is maintained by volunteers.

*Historic Farmington, 3033 Bardstown Rd., Louisville, KY 40205 **Tel:** (502) 452-9920 **Web:** www.farmingtonhistorichomes.org **Open:** Tues.-Sat., 10 a.m. - 4:30 p.m. **Acreage:** garden less than one acre, 18 total **Fee(s):** none for gardens, guided tours **Botanical Collections:** historic flower & herb gardens, orchard.

3. Whitehall House & Gardens
Louisville, Kentucky

Built 1855, the original eight-room two-story red-brick house was remodeled in 1910 into a 15 room, Classical Revival antebellum mansion. A formal Florentine garden recaptures the original design.

*Whitehall House & Gardens, 3110 Lexington Rd., Louisville, KY 40205 **Tel:** (502) 897-2944 **Web:** www.historichomes.org/whitehall **Open:** Mon.- Fri., 10 a.m.-2 p.m. **Acreage:** gardens 2, total 10 **Fee(s):** admission, guided tours **Botanical Collections:** formal Florentine garden.

4. Locust Grove Historic Home
Louisville, Kentucky

This 1790 Georgian plantation house was the last home of Revolutionary War General, George Rogers Clark, a National Register and National Historic Landmark. Period-style gardens with rare and historic plants complement the surrounding landscape of woods and meadows.

*Locust Grove Historic Home, 561 Blankenbaker Lane, Louisville, KY 40207 **Tel:** (502) 897-9845 **Web:** www.locustgrove.org **Open:** Mon.-Sat., 10 a.m.-4:30 p.m., Sun., 1 p.m. - 4:30 p.m. **Acreage:** 55 total **Fee(s):** guided tours **Botanical Collections:** historic period gardens, cutting, formal, herb gardens.

5. Yew Dell Gardens
Crestwood, Kentucky

The former 33-acre estate of Theodore Klein, an avid horticulturalist and commercial nurseryman, serves the Greater Louisville community as a botanic recreational and research asset. Over the six decades that Mr. Klein planted and cultivated the grounds at Yew Dell, he developed an arboretum, a Serpentine Evergreen Garden, holly allee, English Wall Garden and a Secret Garden. The primary focus of Yew Dell Gardens is research, test and display, new plant development, ornamental horticulture and education.

*Yew Dell Gardens, 6220 Old La Grange Rd., P. O. Box 1334, Crestwood, KY 40014 **Tel:** (502) 241-4788 **Web:** www.yewdellgardens.org **Open:** April-Nov., Mon.-Sat., 10 a.m.- 4 p.m.; Dec.-March, Mon.-Fri., 10 a.m.- 4 p.m. **Acreage:** 33 total **Fee(s):** admission fee, plant sales, membership **Botanical Collections:** arboretum, conifer, ferns, perennials, hosta.

6. Bernheim Arboretum & Research Forest
Clermont, Kentucky

Issac Wolfe Bernheim, a German immigrant, established the arboretum in 1929. Kentucky's official arboretum (since 1992) is a nationally recognized 14,000 acre arboretum and research forest preserve; however, only 2,000 acres are developed and opened to the public and 250 acres are designated arboretum. Based on a design by the Frederick Law Olmsted landscape firm, the arboretum includes a visitor center, 35 miles of trails, landscaped gardens, a library, amphitheater, lakes, sculpture, gift shop, café and children's play garden. The arboretum showcases more than 6,000 species of woody plants and herbaceous perennials, native grassland, swamp and natural woodland. Prominent plant collections include holly, nut trees, dogwood, viburnum, ginkgo, maple and crabapple.

*Bernheim Arboretum & Research Forest, SR 245 (25 miles south Louisville on I-65, exit 112), Clermont, KY 40110 **Tel:** (502) 955-8512 **Web:** www.bernheim.org   **Open:** daily, 7 a.m.- sunset, closed Christmas Day and New Year's Day   **Acreage:** 250 arboretum, 14,000 total **Fee(s):** admission on weekends, special events, programs, classes, workshops, membership   **Botanical Collections:** arboretum, perennials, butterfly garden, natives, wetlands.

Purple Redbud, Bernheim Arboretum & Research Forest, Clermont, Kentucky

Helpful Books

Anderton, Stephen. *Urban Sanctuaries: Peaceful Haven for the City Gardener*. Portland, Oregon: Timber Press, 2001.

----------. *Rejuvenating a Garden*. San Francisco, California: Soma Books, 1999.

Andrews, Moya L. *Perennials Short and Tall: A Seasonal Progression of Flowers for Your Garden*. Bloomington: Indiana University Press, 2008.

Bennett, Paul. *The Garden Lover's Guide to the Midwest*. New York: Princeton Architectural Press, 2000.

Brookes, John. *John Brookes' Natural Landscapes*. New York: DK Publishers, 1998.

Canales, Rebecca, Helen Bunnell, and Ann Callow. *Garden Jaunts: A Directory of Gardens and Related Sites in Indiana, Illinois, Michigan and Ohio*. Fort Wayne, Indiana: Foellinger-Freimann Botanical Conservatory, 2002.

Cliff, Stafford. *1,000 Garden Ideas*. London: Quadrille, 2007.

Cohen, Stephanie and Nancy J. Ondra. *The Perennial Gardener's Design Primer: The Essential Guide to Creating Simply Sensational Gardens*. North Adams, Massachusetts: Storey Publishers, 2005.

Dean, Charles and Clyde Wachsberger. *Of Leaf and Flower: Stories and Poems for Gardeners*. New York: Persea Books, 2001.

Douglas, Williams L. *Garden Design: History, Principles, Elements, Practice*. New York: Simon & Schuster, 1984.

Fearnley-Whittingstall, Jane. *The Garden: An English Love Affair: One Thousand Years of Gardening*. London: Weidenfeld & Nicolson, 2002.

Fizzell, James A. *Month-by-Month Gardening in Indiana: What to Do Each Month to Have a Beautiful Garden*. Nashville, Tennessee: Cool Springs Press, 2006.

Gerlach-Spriggs, Nancy, Richard E. Kaufman and Sam Bass Warner. *Restorative Gardens: The Healing Landscape*. New Haven, CT: Yale University Press, 1998.

Haggard, Ezra. *Perennials for the Lower Midwest*. Bloomington: Indiana University Press, 1996.

----------. *Trees, Shrubs & Roses for Midwest Gardens*. Bloomington: Indiana University Press, 2001.

Harstad, Carolyn. *Got Shade: A "Take it Easy" Approach for Today's Gardener.* Bloomington: Indiana University Press, 2003.

------------------. *Go Native: Gardening with Native Plants and Wildflowers.* Bloomington: Indiana University Press, 1999.

Heilenman, Diane. *Gardening in the Lower Midwest: A Practical Guide for the New Zones 5 & 6.* Bloomington: Indiana University Press, 1994.

Hillegass, Linda L. *Flowering Gardening in the Hot Midwest: USDA Zone 5 & Lower Zone 4.* Urbana: University of Illinois Press, 2000.

Jay, Roni. *Gardens of the Spirit: Create Your Own Sacred Spaces.* New York: Sterling Publishers, 1998.

Lacy, Allen. *The Inviting Garden: Gardening for the Senses, Mind and Spirit.* New York: Henry Holt, 1998.

Marranca, Bonnie. *American Garden Writing: An Anthology.* Lanham, Maryland: Taylor Trade Publishing, 2003.

Martin, Laura C. and Allen Rokach. *Gardens of the Heartland.* New York: Abbeville Press, 1996.

Oguchi, Motomi, Joseph Cali and Kay Yokota. *Create Your Own Japanese Garden: A Practical Guide.* Tokyo: Kodansha International, 2007.

Olson, Marsha. *A Garden of Love & Healing: Living Tributes to Those We Have Loved & Lost.* Minneapolis, Minnesota: Fairview Press, 2002.

Ondra, Nancy J. and Stephanie Cohen. *Fallscaping: Extending Your Garden Season into Autumn.* North Adams, Massachusetts: Storey Publishers, 2007.

Otis, Denise. *Grounds for Pleasure: Four Centuries of the American Garden.* New York: Harry N. Abrams, 2002.

Ross, Stephanie. *What Gardening Means.* Chicago: University of Chicago Press, 1998.

Sharp, Jo Ellen and Tom Tyler. *Indiana Gardener's Guide.* Nashville, Tennessee: Cool Springs Press, 2004.

Turner, Tom. *Garden History: Philosophy and Design, 2000 BC-2000 AD.* London: Spon Press, 2005.

INDEX

125